Judo inside out

Geof Gleeson

JUDO inside out

A Cultural reconciliation

Lepus Books

First published 1983 by Lepus Books, an imprint of
EP Publishing Limited, Bradford Road, East Ardsley,
Wakefield, West Yorkshire WF3 2JN

Copyright © 1983 Geof Gleeson

All rights reserved. No part of this publication may be
reproduced, stored in a retrieval system, or transmitted,
in any way or by any means, electronic, mechanical,
photocopying, recording or otherwise, without the prior
permission of EP Publishing Limited.

Phototypeset by The Word Factory,
Accrington, Lancashire

Printed and bound by Butler & Tanner Limited
Frome, Somerset

British Library Cataloguing in Publication Data

Gleeson, Geof
  Judo inside out
  1. Judo
  I. Title
  796.8'152   GV1114

ISBN 0 86019 100 1
(Cased Edition)

ISBN 0 86019 108 7
(Limp Edition)

Contents

Foreword, 11

Acknowledgements, 12

Introduction, 13

Chapter 1 **Some Differences between Skill and Technique**, 19

Chapter 2 **Countering Skills**, 41

Chapter 3 **Let's Start Again**, 55

Chapter 4 **The Psychology of Competition – or How to Make the Most out of Very Little**, 73

Chapter 5 **A Picture is Worth a Thousand Words**, 103

Chapter 6 **A Summing Up**, 137

Glossary, 142

Notes and Bibliography, 145

Index, 153

Foreword

The higher echelons of coaching have been extraordinarily fortunate to have experienced the seminal influence of Geof Gleeson this past quarter-century. 'A dwarf on the shoulders of a giant sees further than the giant': I have often been that dwarf on the author's shoulders, and yet, when I have stepped down again there has never been any trace of condescension in the continued guidance. There is no trace of condescension in this book.

Bernard Shaw said, 'The reasonable man adapts himself to the world; the unreasonable man persists in trying to adapt the world to himself. Therefore, all progress is made by the unreasonable man.' Geof Gleeson is both a reasonable and unreasonable man; by bringing his wide experience of life as both a top judo player and a top judo coach, together with his vast knowledge of eastern, western, marxist, christian and other philosophies on sport/judo, to bear upon the matters discussed in this book, he has prepared the way for the unreasonable man to progress and the reasonable man to adapt.

St Francis preached on the edge of the pool and the fishes said how beautiful and logical were his words and then went away and swam around as they had always done. Few are ever persuaded by argument; readers of this book, though they may change their views not at all, will see what is in their muddy pool far more clearly.

John Crooke, Shrewsbury, March 1982
Former Secretary, British Association of National Coaches
Former Director of Coaches' Training,
The Professional Tennis Coaches' Association of Great Britain
Twice British Professional Tennis Men's Doubles Champion

Acknowledgements

My first thanks go to Colin McIver, the Editor of the national judo magazine, for providing all the action photographs in Chapter 5. He also took them. Many thanks too to Brian Daley for helping me pose the stills in the same chapter – despite his protests that the pictures would look 'silly'! I agreed with him and we did have some difficulty looking so motionless, but the distinction between action and posed pictures was important and fundamental to the text. Philip Harrison had the uninspiring task of taking these photographs. He too has my thanks.

Many of the ideas contained in the text were those created during my research time at the Polytechnic of North London. It was a very exhilarating time, studying full-time subject areas that previously had only been touched on in spare-time moments. In its own particular way this time compared favourably with my study time in Japan, the practical source of so many of my ideas on judo coaching that I have implemented since then. I am most grateful to the P.N.L. for giving me such an opportunity for theoretical study and to the Japanese family Takasaki for the opportunity to do the practical work at length.

I must thank too my publishers for the support they have given me and the editors and designers who have done so much to make the book look good – an important element in any text-book of this kind; also the British Museum, for kind permission to reproduce the Kuniyoshi print on the jacket.

Lastly, but only last because she is always there, I must acknowledge my unrepayable debt to my wife, not only official typist, strict proof-reader, capable improver of style, but staunch supporter in all things. A thank-you can never be enough.

G.R.G. May 1982

Introduction

Judo was born in Japan a hundred years ago, in the land of the rising sun, a part of that world of mystery known as the Orient; a mystery created by Kipling, Maugham, Lafcadio Hearn and Dr Fu Man Chu. Paradox and ambiguity is expected from it and if they are not there, the West will inject some of its own. When something appears simple the West will make it complicated; when complicated it is made simple. Judo exploitation is an excellent example of this intellectual game of inside out. Take a simple act like falling over: any child can do it, but in judo it is raised to an art form – the Art of Falling; whereas something as difficult and as complicated as a competitive fighting skill is reduced to a technique that simply needs repetition to make it effective. Such a strange attitude is bound to develop strange practices and judo abounds in them. But it must be conceded that it is not helped by the foreign culture that is Japan. The oriental thinking is so different that great effort must be made to accommodate it. When I teach Japanese I always make the point in the first lesson that it is not the learning of the vocabulary and the grammar that is difficult, but understanding the concepts behind the words. So many of the things appear inside out to western minds. For example, the Japanese carpenter's saw cuts on the up-stroke and clears on the down-stroke, the Japanese house has the roof built first and the walls filled in after. So when I teach judo I have repeatedly to make the point that much of its practices have become confused because of this same lack of conceptual understanding behind the judo terminology, and therefore they must be prepared for paradox and ambivalence in the training. By turning some of these attitudes inside out, to look at the concepts from a completely different point of view, perhaps some of these mysteries may become less mysterious and the elementary more obvious.

To start as we intend to go on, let us ask what is the nature of judo? Judo when talked about by judo people is always treated as an 'individual sport', meaning that it is a sport for the individual not for a team. Well, perhaps it is not a team sport, like football, but it is certainly a group sport. No individual can do judo on his own; he needs the support and assistance of a whole army of people to help him to do his 'thing'. Not only is a partner or opponent obviously essential, but there are also all those fellow trainees who provide the opposition for him to sharpen his skills upon and offer him advice and help on how to improve his performance. Then there is the coach and/or a teaching staff, plus an organising group that includes secretaries, treasurers, committee members, and last, but by no means least, that band of referees, judges, time-keepers, all of whom the individual judo player cannot do without. Certainly Kano saw judo as a community-orientated activity rather than an individual-orientated one; this is shown clearly by his maxim, 'ji ta kyo ei',* and is elaborated on extensively in his writings.

To participate in judo the individual will generally approach it through some group, either parents or friends. Such friends frequently take him to the judo group or introduce him in some other way, so the first of many judo expectations experienced by an individual will not be received from the judo group itself but from outside it. Such expectations, however seemingly ephemeral, will influence how that individual approaches the task of learning judo. Then, once in the judo group, the expectations and ideologies of the group will quickly impinge on the individual and he will need to compromise them with those he learnt earlier. After a short time, when his ability begins to make an appearance, he will become aware of other groups – the national governing body for example – and these too will affect how he learns, when he learns and what he learns. When he begins to compete seriously he will find himself having to deal with even further distant groups – but nevertheless important ones – the spectators, the media people and others. No, judo cannot be called an individual sport. It really is a group sport for not only are the competitive skills affected by these groups but many kinds of responsibilities and obligations will be generated by the relationships with those groups, which the individual must – or at least should – recognise and accept.

Having said that, it is quite understandable why judo has been seen as an individual sport. The competitive, sporting, aspect of judo has been defined by those throwing and grappling skills which

---

* It is curious to notice that when the Japanese translate this maxim into English they invariably omit the 'ji ta', and some British, since the last war, seem to have forgotten what it means.

appear to need only one man to do them. And this impression is strengthened when these skills are simplified further by treating them as techniques needing only one or two men to accomplish them. Once that attitude is accepted the next step towards over-individualisation comes when those techniques are treated as bottle-necks preventing developments into the broader ranges of skill acquisition, instead of narrow passes between technical and social skills, through which the performer frequently has to travel in both directions.

It is also of course so much easier to talk about and teach techniques because photographs of them can be taken, diagrams drawn and sequences of movements described. Group interactions are so much more difficult to represent. Some special types of diagram can be drawn but on the whole the phenomenon is abstract and impossible to represent by diagrams or photographs. So I will have to write about these interactions as provocatively as I can and then if the reader is interested he/she can follow the subject up in the reading material I have included in the bibliography at the back of the book.§

The metaphysical point I am trying to make is that technique cannot be treated in isolation as all judo text-books do, for there are many many other things which affect and modify all techniques when they are converted into a competitive skill. I will try to indicate some of these influences as a 'By the way' to be found scattered throughout the book: these are notes that are not directly related to the practical part, but contain an indirect influence that I consider to be important. However, somewhere has to be selected as a place to start from, so in this one instance I shall be conventional and choose the conventional place to start – technique. To facilitate this initial discussion let me tabulate and clarify the terminology – or the jargon – I shall be using to describe offensive and defensive movements contained within the constraints of a skill.

An attack. An offensive action, in standing or ground grappling, that is intended to elicit a defensive reaction from the opponent, or make a winning score; in practice it may not achieve either.

A right/left-handed throw. The direction in which the opponent falls – to his right side or left side – determines the title of the

---

§ When this mark is found it means that there is a 'further reading' section in the bibliography.

throw. In the following text all the throws described are right-handed unless otherwise stated.

An attacking movement. Refers generally to the movement necessary to get from the 'stand-off' position (i.e. in a standing-grappling situation) to a place where the attacker can make the throwing movement. The movements consist of the following parts:

Pivot foot/leg: the right foot is moved to an attacking position, the left foot swings, pivots, about that right foot into a position where it becomes the ...

Driving foot/leg: the left leg drives the whole attacker's body-weight into the direction of the throw. It should be noted this is not the only way to make an attacking movement, but it is the most effective.

Grip/hand-hold. The orthodox grip is: left hand holds partner's right sleeve, right hand holds opponent's collar (therefore left hand = sleeve-hand, right hand = collar hand); in practice judo players will vary this grip considerably.

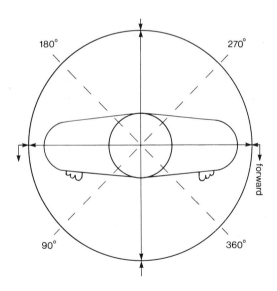

Throwing directions, top view of opponent.

Line of attack. Refers to the direction of the attack made on the opponent: usually it is straight from the front but occasionally it is, and can be, varied by changing the position of the feet (before the attack is launched) so that the line of attack can be from the (opponent's) sides or oblique front.

Direction of throw. Refers to the direction in which the attacker wants to throw the opponent: it can, but does not have to, line up with the line of attack; usually range is 270° (see diagram opposite), but it can be 360°; standard throws like *uchimata* throw anywhere in the first two quadrants (180°), *seoinage* can cover three quadrants (270°), whereas throws like *kouchi* and *kosoto* can range through the third and fourth quadrants (360°).

Opportunity. The 'trigger' that starts an attack may be a particular body-shape made by the opponent; it can be forced by the attacker through the use of tactics, or the opponent can make a mistake which creates an opportunity; it is better if the opportunity is forced because the attacker cannot always wait until a mistake is made – it may never happen!

When talking about simple attacks, just one attempt at a throw, it is fairly simple to differentiate between the attacker and the attacked (but even then not always); but once complex attacks are being analysed it can be very confusing. So I am using my own terms because I am assuming that the man being attacked is the weaker (less skilful) of the two and hence will be the centre of the action: he will be–

The target (in Japanese *uke*). But his is not the passive role. He is very much aware that he is the target and is able to move about aggressively both to avoid the attacks and/or stop them. When some elementary abstract situation is being discussed the name 'attacker', or 'defender' will be used in a passive way to indicate that the situation is not a real one.*

The target is of course the objective of –

The hit-man (in Japanese *tori*). He is the slightly better performer, both in terms of experience and skill, so he invariably sets the conditions of the match and the target has to respond as best he can; when the situation is not real, he will be known simply as the 'partner' or the 'opponent'.

---

* Most judo text-books talk about the opponent as if he had not a thought in his head.

It is understood, I hope, that all the above terms will apply equally in ground grappling. By and large standing-grappling is so much more dynamic and exciting than ground-grappling, that it is to be expected that it needs a greater range of terminology to cover all eventualities. However, ground-grappling will need – at some time – all the same terms.

So now let's get to it – turn as much as possible inside out and see what falls out!

Chapter 1
Some Differences between Skill and Technique

'The Technical Commission was in session. It had been told to compile a grading syllabus, but the purpose for it had not been given. After much confused discussion, confused because no-one knew what they were doing, or more to the point why they were doing it, they agreed to a "shopping list" of techniques. The Commission said (with a note of some reticence) that if the shapes of these techniques were known properly they would eventually turn into a skill.'

Let me admit straight away that I am not starting at the beginning. I am not going to describe how a novice starts learning judo (that is in Chapter 3), I am going to start a considerable way along the learning path, for I want to make it clear at the outset what I consider judo skills to be, before I try to describe ways of achieving them. In addition to that I want to emphasise that not only are skills different from techniques, but the same skills are different from the same skills – that is, different people will do the same skills in different ways.

In the past, and present too, the novice is indoctrinated with the word 'technique'. Not only are all beginners' courses filled with 'technique', but so too are the grading syllabuses (those 'shopping lists' that are supposed to improve skills if they are learnt by rote). Technique thus becomes the major factor in the novice's learning programme and, as many psychologists acknowledge, what is learnt early in the process of skill acquisition remains critically significant until way past the skill's peak.§ Yet of necessity, in practice, tech-

---

§ When this mark is found, it means that there is a 'further reading' section in the bibliography.

nique must be superseded by skill. Technique is never sufficient to cope with the complexities of a competitive situation, until and unless it has evolved into a skill. Therefore because skill is the eventual objective of training, I want to bring it much further forward – introduce it earlier – in the training programme, and have it presented (to the performer) in such a way that he understands it better and thus perhaps learns it more quickly.

Technique and skill

First I must make some attempt to define and differentiate skill and technique.§ As a start may I offer a definition of technique: it is the use of the body and its bits and pieces (arms, legs and head) to transmit force to the opponent, in order to bring about some pre-determined effect, i.e. make him fall down, pin him to the ground or break his arm. In order to appreciate and understand the function of technique, it is best learnt in the simplest of circumstances, i.e. in a non-varying situation, standing or lying still. Skill is the application and therefore the adaptation of technique to an ever-differing situation; it is implicit that maximum consistency of success is desirable when learning the necessary modifications.

In training technique and skill must be learnt; the questions to be asked are when and how are they to be taught? There is no finite answer, it will depend upon the nature of the learning group. However, what is important is to realise that there is no sacrosanct order of presentation. Technique does not *have* to precede skill (as it always has done in the judo world); a simplified form of skill can be taught first, followed by technique (see Chapter 3). Not every group need be taught the same way: the aspirations of the individuals should decide the form of teaching as it does the style of learning.

How does a technique become a skill?

In a judo competition each individual is trying to impose his skill upon the other, with the intention of winning (as specified by the rules). For this to happen each competitor must be able to assess what the opposition has, both in the sense of attack and defence, and how that will integrate with his own strengths and weaknesses. Most judo text-books, if they attempt to describe how this can be done (which few do), would give the analysis from the hit-man's point of view. I want to adopt the opposite approach; I want to make the analysis from the target's point of view. I chose this approach for the following reasons:

Some Differences between Skill and Technique   21

1. An efficient fighter always assumes he is the weaker in skills (not the weaker in determination to win). It may not be true, but in this way he will not underestimate the opposition.
2. Accepting an inferior – but temporary – relationship makes the necessity of correct analysis more pressing and essential to get right.
3. Being weaker than the opposition is a common relationship often found in any fighter's career, yet seldom discussed. For some strange reason it is always suggested that the fighter should assume he is the better man when working out tactics. I say strange because in any championship there is only one winner, the rest are losers, so there must be a lot more 'weaker-relationships' than 'stronger-relationships'.

Because by definition skill is the adaptation to an ever-changing set of circumstances, it is impossible to describe any specific skill in general terms. Therefore let me try to give some particular examples, with some general hints for possible practical analysis. I will start with the technique and then look at some of the ways it can be modified when put to the test of competition.

Some examples

Let me take as the first example that maid-of-all-work *taiotoshi*, (fig. 1 shows it as a technique; see p.105). The forces being applied to the opponent are through hands – pushing forward, through the hips (as they rotate forward and down), through the driving (left) leg – thrusting both bodies forward. The attacker gets to this position by stepping forward (right foot first, left foot back, which also turns the body), right leg moved into the blocking position. Done in a co-operative, structured circumstance the movement and the technique is quite simple and well within the capabilities of most sportspeople.

The skill of *taiotoshi* may well vary tremendously from what has been described above. How would the target start to decide what the opponent's *taiotoshi* is going to look like, assuming that he knows the attack will be *taiotoshi*?*

As the contest is in weight classes, the opposition is of course of much the same body-weight, but how is that weight distributed? Is he

---

* Most good-class competitors have only one or two winning skills, which are generally well known. If his style is not known (he is a 'new face') then his opposition would no doubt have studied his performance in preliminary matches and films.

tall and (comparatively) thin or short and (comparatively) round? If tall, it will be a very 'leggy' *taiotoshi*: a long leg quickly pushed across, probably very low (about ankle height). If short, a very 'hippy' *taiotoshi*, the attacker's bottom in very deep (no leg contact at all).

Is his movement quality fast/jerky or slow/smooth? If fast, the attacker may not bother to turn as he makes the attack, simply sticking the leg quickly across; the throwing direction may even be backwards. If slow, he will turn the full 180°, making sure he can compensate for any loss of control by application of maximum power.

Are the hands active or passive? If they are working all the time – pulling, pushing, twisting, together, separately – they will probably try for a quick reaction. The target can expect to get some sharp bang in the chest, or a poke in the ribs: if he responds unthinkingly to such provocation the attack will be launched before he knows he has responded. If the hit-man's hands stay mostly still during standing-grappling, they may not move until after an attack has started. The hips will move smoothly into position and only then will the hands start their job of pushing.

What sort of tactics is the hit-man using? Does he act defensively much of the time (staying in a deep, difficult crouch), only occasionally attacking in a really 'kami-kaze' manner? Is he very fast, very aggressive, depending on a drastic change of pace to compensate for his very poor technique? Is he a change-of-direction man? As he moves about the contest area is he continually changing direction abruptly and in a very – apparently – disjointed manner? If so, the attack will be made on one of the changes of direction.

The target has much to think about. If he has trained correctly he will depend upon his kinesthetic thinking rather than his verbal thinking, but whatever the mind-body process is, some kind of thinking must be happening in order to decide what must be done. There will be, of course, many subtle variations between these extreme examples I have given of *taiotoshi*. Providing the target understands that the *taiotoshi* that is going to be aimed at him will have very little – if any – similarities with the *taiotoshi* technique he learnt on his beginners' course, he may have a good chance of beating it (see Chapter 2).

Next let us have a look at the cautious man's favourite attack, *osotogake*. The technique is as follows: the right leg is hooked in tightly behind the opposition's right knee, pulling back and up; but first the feet step into position, right foot first, left foot back near

Some Differences between Skill and Technique 23

partner's left foot; hands twist the shoulders. Done this way it is easily appreciated why cautious players like it. They can abandon the attack at virtually any stage – even after the right leg has hooked in; because the body does not need to turn, the attacker can watch the opposition throughout the attack. It is an attack, however, that is easily countered if the attacker's left foot is carelessly placed.

The skills of *osotogake* are almost – but not quite – as various as *taiotoshi*. Certainly the direction of the throw can vary enormously (the back 180°) which means the positioning of the left foot can vary to the same extent (see fig. 23-27, p.118-120). Hands can pull up, down or round. So the target will again have to look at the opposition's height. If tall, hands could pull up, if short round or down (sometimes even up). Supple opposition may sweep hips, not the leg at all: stiff opponents may hack at the Achilles tendon. The target may find a shoulder rammed in his teeth – to get his head back; he may find almost no tension on his right sleeve at all, much to his discomposure, but a crisp poke under the lobe of his left ear will remind him what is important in this kind of attack – making the target's head go down, so that in turn it makes the body posture bend towards the ground. The opportunity to attack may come in any direction of movement – when the target is moving backwards, sideways or circular. The target may find himself 'bounced' off the edge of the contest area. Having sussed out what this particular hit-man has got, the target must be prepared to move, to duck under the enthusiastic jabbing left hand, to move in close to the long-limbed, to move away from the short-legged. As he finds himself moving backwards towards the edge of the contest area, the target will prepare to come away from the edge in a totally unexpected way.

As the last illustration, let us look at some ground-grappling (*ne-waza*). Look at the technique of a mid-side pin (*kuzure-kami-shihogatame*, fig. 46 on p. 131). The attacker's weight is on the opponent's right shoulder, feet/legs spread wide for stability, head held high – to keep force on shoulders, and to see what's going on. Hands pull in tight, ensuring there is no gap between the bodies. It all looks very innocuous and simple.

The skill of a mid-upper pin is something else. The target finds that not only is his shoulder being weighted down but so is his head! His chest will feel as if it is being crushed, slowly, everything is most uncomfortable, difficulty in breathing, aches everywhere; what should he be looking for so that by attacking such points he can return the aches? For a start he will need to look for the same things as when he is standing-grappling, waiting to be hit by his opponent. The long man will tend to have his weight low, the legs extended (the leg-weight far from the target's body then brings a useful anchoring leverage). The body will tend to stay more or less in the same place with the hands also staying in much the same place but pulling in tight. The short hit-man will tend to carry his weight high, with legs much closer to the target's body. This will mean he can move quickly (either to change attacks or retain position). The hands may change position several times (for control usually, but sometimes it is simply a fidgety action). Legs too will change fairly frequently (crossing and uncrossing), mainly because – with the weight being high – the general position is more unstable. The short legs will be used much more as stabilisers than the long legs. So the target will feel in the one situation – of the long man – a fairly fixed and clamping/pressing weight, or – in the case of the short man – he may feel a fairly mobile weight, apparently easy enough to move, but in practice difficult to counter-attack because of its very mobility. The shorter man will tend to hustle and create his opportunities by forcing the target man to move too fast and so make mistakes. The long man will tend to impose opportunities simply by forcing the target into certain positions that the long man knows he can exploit.

So it becomes apparent that even what may appear to be a fairly limited situation, a mid-upper pin, in practice provides a wide range of variations for the target to appreciate and catalogue in his thinking-file system. For simplicity's sake I have made long and short competitors prefer certain types of body movement; obviously in practice these preferences may well be mixed up. What is to be appreciated is that different types of people produce different types of skill.

A by the way

Let me take a break here from discussing specific viewpoints of technique and skills and look briefly at whether there is any advantage or benefit in having a technique-dominated early training period. For example, does a grading syllabus full of techniques facilitate the acquisition of skills? It will of course depend on how it is used. Most extant grading syllabuses use a standard technique as a template against which reproductions of other techniques are compared. If there is a slight deviation the performance is judged as incorrect and is penalised accordingly. In my opinion this is quite the wrong way to use a syllabus. It stultifies any ability and it produces an attitude in the trainee that assumes there is only one way

Some differences between Skill and Technique 25

to perform a technique or skill. This approach will destroy – and has destroyed – skills. If, however, a syllabus is used as a starting point, a form that provides a stimulus for personal development, then it has much value. Instead of asking the normal, debilitating syllabus question 'What is *taiotoshi*?', and expecting to see an exact replication of some diagram printed on some sheet of paper, the question that should be asked is, 'How many different forms of *taiotoshi* can you demonstrate?' That would be so much the more constructive way of using a syllabus. From the outset of learning this would help to produce in the coaching fraternity a structured approach to teaching. It would not be good enough for a coach to 'pass on' some over-simplified arbitrary version of a technique, he would (one hopes) have to learn how variations of technique came about. Structured learning means of course *kata* (more about this in Chapter 4), which would mean that syllabus-technique would encourage, indirectly, the expansion of the *kata*-concept within the training programme.

The same applies when considering technique-dominated beginners' courses. Working on the assumption that learning has to start somewhere, the provision of a standard performance is as good a way of starting as any. However, the proviso is, as no doubt the reader will by now anticipate, that such a convenience is not held up to be the last word on performance. If the single-technique is used as a common starting point, just as the multi-technique of the *randori-no-kata* could be used as a starting point for the development of individual skills, all will be well. If techniques are used as constraints on skill development, they will destroy the sport of judo.

A return to techniques and skill

Here are three more different forms of conversions of techniques into skills. After that, perhaps the reader will be able to make his own comments on competitive evolution.

Fig. 43 (p.129) shows a typical foot-trip. There are many versions of this basic idea, which is to knock the legs out from under the opposition. In simplistic terms there are two forms: one where a foot or leg is literally kicked out from underneath a person and the other where a foot or leg is prevented from moving and the person made to fall over it. The attacker blocks the opponent's right foot with his left, the opponent's right arm is pulled well forward, turning his shoulders and so making him fall forward over his trapped foot. The attacker's pushing right hand will also reinforce this turning action. The attacker's body-twist will supplement the turning action, driving the opponent over the trapped foot.

In the skilled performance, the target will need to expect every possible deviation from the above standard technique. The attack can be made on either the sleeve- or the collar-side: the trapping action can happen at any place from knee to toes (occasionally even as high as the hip); the twisting action can be to the front or the back, the pulls and pushes can be down, up, forward or backward.

The target will probably find the long man pulling up and possibly pushing backwards (getting very close to *kosotogari*). The tall/fast attacker may pull up and throw so far forward that the target will have little chance of touching the ground till he lands on his back (see p.57). The short/fast man may try to pull the head down low, twist to the side and fall over the target (getting very close to *sutemi-waza*). The short/slow man may pull the right sleeve down and push up with his right hand. The direction again could vary from side to back. Opportunities and pace when considered can also vary tremendously. The target can be hit when he is standing still or moving fast – and anywhere in between; when he is moving forward, backwards, sideways – or in circles. He must always be ready for the whistling, scything foot of the hit-man, coming at him at any time, any place. If he ever adopts an indifferent attitude to foot trip attacks he will either end up on his back or find great bruises on his legs.

Next, a back-throw (*seoinage*) – Fig. 10.* Notice particularly the position of the feet, in relation to the partner's: the hips are in very deep, ensuring that the partner is rotated over the back (hence the name of the throw). The hands are used, essentially, to pull the partner's head down in order to facilitate the rotation across the back.

When the target is looking for the back-throw, again he must expect every possible permutation of factors. The hit-man can attack from the outset with only one hand holding: usually it is the collar-hand that is freed (*ippon-seoinage*), but it has been known for the sleeve-hand to be freed. The hips can be thrust in very deep: again it has been known for supple hit-men to get their hips behind the target (and throw him backwards). As for the legs, sometimes the attacker can drop on both knees, sometimes he will keep his legs straight – right from the beginning. The direction of throw can vary through

---

* For some strange reason this throw has always been known in judo circles as a shoulder-throw. It is very misleading because the throw has little to do with the shoulders and even the Japanese name means 'to carry on the back'.

270°, from backwards to the target's left side.

It is virtually impossible to say who – in terms of type – will prefer what permutation of factors. For the sake of giving examples I have assembled body types to a particular set of factors, but in practice I can think of exceptions to every combination.

The tall/flexible man may throw the target to his right, with no – or very little – bend in his legs. He will simply roll the target across his back. The tall/stiff man may only push his right hip into body-contact and then depend upon the leverage from the limb length to pull the target up and round the small of his back. The short/supple hit-man may aim to get his bottom between the legs of the target and lift from there, while the short/stiff attacker will try for a fairly standard version – hips moderately deep (half-way), legs half bent, hands driving forward.

The opportunity of course will vary tremendously, everything again from the static situation to high-speed convolutions. The target can expect to be attacked at any time by a *seoinage* hit-man, whether he is going backwards, forward, sideways or in a circle. When opportunity is linked with direction of throw, there are many permutations. The target must be very alert and have his wits about him at all times when fighting a *seoinage* opponent. Those wits will need be kept so that hopefully the attack can be stopped before it starts. Those same wits must be prepared to save the day when the target finds himself flying through the air for a terminal score. As he so flies he must be able to twist or turn in such a way that he does not land on his back. It is very important for any competitor to remember

> He that twists
> and avoids a ten score
> lives to fight
> a great deal more.

Finally in this section, let us look at a straight arm-lock (fig. 49, p.132: *juji-gatame*). Notice both the attacker's legs are across the opponent's body, so giving as much control over him as possible. It also allows the attacker's thighs to get close to the body and so act as a fulcrum over which the arm will be bent.

The application of *juji-gatame* can vary little whether it is a skill or a technique. However, either thigh of course can be used as a fulcrum, and sometimes both legs are not put across the opponent, but only one (control does tend to diminish if this is done). What does vary considerably is the approach to the application. Unfortunately, in most learning situations for novices, the victim is shown lying on his back and the attacker moves in and always ends up in the position shown in fig. 48 (p.132). Again in competition the target must expect this arm-lock to be applied at any time – when he is standing up, on his hands and knees, lying face down as well as face up. As for the hit-man, he knows that it takes a comparatively long time to get into the right technical position (i.e. legs across body, arm out straight etc.) so he will use diversionary attacks, or opportunities that are so 'wrong' that the target does not expect such an attack to be made.

For example, when both competitors are in vertical-grappling but crouched and moving very slowly and strongly, it has been known for one man to stand quickly (with one foot) on the thigh of the opponent, swing the other's leg up, over and around the opponent's head, and drive him backwards, so that he sits down backwards, rolls onto his back and finds himself in the orthodox, final, *juji-gatame* position. The starting position is so completely unsuitable for *juji-gatame* that the target seldom realises what is happening until it is too late. Or, the target can be crouched, tightly defensive, on his elbows and knees; again there seems little danger of *juji-gatame* in this position. But the hit-man slides an arm into the crook of the elbow, throws a leg across and applies the arm-lock whilst he is still crouching. So again the target must not expect a standard situation.

The tall/flexible man may well try the lock when he has just scored a 3 or 5 throwing attack and the target is about to reach, or is on his way to, a standing position. A fast step in, the long leg is thrown over the body and head and again the target has got problems. So whenever the target is changing position he should be on the look-out for any attack from the hit-man – it will come from any angle at any time.

A by the way

When investigators are looking into natural phenomena there is a tendency to classify or categorise whatever discoveries they make during the investigation.§ This taxonomic propensity serves two main functions; it is a shorthand of convenience for both reference and understanding (and is the origin of jargon), and an attempt to inject some sort of reason into what invariably looks like chaos in the natural state. The danger with such an approach (as always when establishing initial symbolic imagery) is that the classification can itself become sacrosanct; not only is it assumed to be the only way of categorising the phenomenon, but sometimes the phenomenon *becomes* the categorisation.§

Traditional judo classification of throwing techniques rests upon the criteria of body parts (legs, hands, hips etc.) Presumably this was because Kano considered body-mechanism as the most axiomatic aspect of analysis to stress at that time. However, it does not appear that he gave the criteria much importance for he makes no attempt to utilise the same elements when analysing ground-grappling techniques (*katame-waza*). The inference is that it was more a convenience of the obvious than the relevancy of the parts. Taking a longer view, particularly when considering skills in competition, perhaps other criteria could be made more relevant, for example stability.

Winning matches is very much a gambling affair. The competitor looks at the many factors and elements within the combat situation, assesses them as best he can (depending on his knowledge and experience), makes a judgement as to what his tactics will be and then gambles on whether he made the right judgement by putting his tactics into operation.§ Like any good gambler, however, he tries to get as much of the odds onto his side as he can before the gamble starts.* Therefore when the fighter selects a throwing technique he could use stability and range of use as his criteria. (Stability referring here to whether he is standing on one or two legs while making the throwing effort). A one-legged throw (e.g. *haraigoshi, hanegoshi, osotogari*) is easily countered (see Chapter 2) because of its one-legged base. This is why the most popular throws – ones like *taiotoshi, seoinage, osotogake* – are two legs/feet on the ground: they are much harder to counter because of their very stable attacking position. Exceptions to the rules, which are few (e.g. *uchimata, ouchigari*) are those that have a high ballistic element. Once having started them, the momentum that is quickly generated is enough to reduce (but not eliminate) the risks of countering.

The other criterion, range of use, refers to scope of application. The more variations there are, the more errors the technique can absorb – and still function – the more the practical fighter will like them. Hence the popularity of *taiotoshi* and *seoinage*. Those techniques are very tolerant of mistakes, they can be done in almost any situation in almost any way – very badly! Conversely, those techniques that have little tolerance of poor skill are not very popular. Techniques like *deashiharai* (often tried, but seldom successful), *osotogari, yoko-sutemi-waza*, are typical of such movements.

---

* As Damon Runyon so aptly put it, 'the race is not always to the swift, or the battle to the strong, but that's the way to bet'.

When analysing ground-grappling techniques (*katame-waza*) the same two criteria of stability and range of use can be utilised. Stability here refers to the approach and application of technique. For example, strangles from the front (e.g. *kata-hajime, nami-jujijime*) are seldom, if ever, used because the attacker's hands have to be near the centre of the body (the opponent's neck). It is a very unstable position and can easily be turned by an aggressive target. Pinning attacks are of course very stable in terms of both approach and application, hence their domination of *katame-waza* tactics. Considering range of use, again the pins (*osaekomi-waza*) appeal very highly in relation to toleration of mistakes and scope of application. Equally the strangles are very intolerant of error and have to be done very accurately or there is no effect.

As a training programme develops, other criteria for categorisation would no doubt be needed. The more obvious ones could be: amount of movement needed to attack (with particular reference to the contest area edge); the ability to link with other attacking skills; the amount of power necessary to make the skills work; the degree of fashion in the skill. The last criterion is a good example of an obtuse influence on skill performance. There are fashions in sports skills just as there are in all branches of man's creativity; what the top fighter or top coach has to decide at some particular point in time (and it may happen several times in one competitor's career) is, will it be better to follow fashion or to break it? If the fashion is just coming in (related to judo it would be some particular skill – like doing *taiotoshi* in a particular way), it may be better to follow fashion. If it is on its way out, then it may be better to break the fashion and start a new one. The tough decision for the coach or performer is, when is the fashion coming and when is it going.

Some other consideratons that will influence training schemes
Camera cautions

In Chapter 5 there is a scatter of action photographs. They are grouped under the headings of stable and unstable attacks. The experienced performers and coaches can enjoy themselves by giving orthodox Japanese names to them and then comparing them with a friend's attempt. Are the results the same?

Unfortunately, with still photographs there is a mass of limitations that restrict analysis: there is no indication of pre-attack movement (naturally), no sign of an opportunity and no indication of the speed of movement when the attack was launched.§ In addition to that there is the bias of the photographer to take into account. Why did he take that particular attack? Does he try and take every throw that is made or does he select? If he selects, on what basis does he select? When a known skilful performer comes onto the mat does the cameraman think: 'Now I'll get a good picture'? When a clumsy (but effective) performer comes onto the mat does he say, 'This man always does "bad" throws so I will not take pictures of him.' If the picture catches the start of a throw, how does it end? These are all questions and problems that impinge on the task of 'translating' action pictures. So although a camera may not tell a lie, it certainly can be 'heard' in many different ways.§

Should tactical plans be made?

It must be conceded immediately that the existing rules of competitive judo in no way encourage the development of tactical skills. The 'sudden death' concept that was and is the essence of these rules has no origin in a traditional British sport ethic, but is an out-dated feudal concept from Japan. Kano himself did not like this and much preferred the 'best out of three points' approach to a competition and it was this method of scoring that was used up until and just after his death. (It was used in Britain for a short time after the Second World War.) By the 1930s the Japanese army had begun to push its bellicose nose into sport; by sponsoring groups (clubs)* throughout the country it was able to inject its objectives into them.§ The army preferred and imposed the 'sudden death' scoring on judo because it manifested the 'old *samurai* spirit'. So as a means to some defunct fascist ideal the 1-point terminal score may have had some value, but as a means of developing a morale and training ethos for a contemporary society it has no place and little value.

Having said that, the fact remains that the contemporary judo performer is faced with a 1-point-only match. In such a contest it is possible to win by doing nothing. If the win-at-all-cost performer plays very defensively, so that he does not give a 10-score away, and his opponent is penalised for making some silly mistake (like putting a foot inadvertently outside the contest area), he can win a major international title. In that case, why should he bother to waste

---

* Nakamura in his book *Supotsu to wa Nanika* (Popura Sha, 1979) suggests there is no Japanese equivalent of a British sports club. Like sport itself, 'club' is a product of a culture that the Japanese do not really understand.§

valuable training time learning difficult, involved, tactical skills? So what follows is really only for those performers and coaches who see the mastery of skills as a challenge in itself and the achievement of them as an excitement which compensates for the drudgery of the competitive event. However, if tactical skills are learnt in the training programme, they are bound to make a significant contribution to any victory, so the learning of them will undoubtedly benefit the ambitious performer.

Some special factors for consideration when planning tactics

Is there such a thing as a sport personality? This can mean, do certain people have innate propensities to be top sportspeople? The answer chosen will go a long way towards deciding what are, if any, the special factors. As with most metaphysical questions there is no definitive answer. Some authorities state categorically that there is, others – equally positive – say of course not. The individual answerer can but allow his prejudice full reign, but hopefully it is one of those better, more educated prejudices that has had its regular intake of substantial knowledge.§

When faced with an alternative of this kind I find the inferred choice is no choice; it only clouds the problem and creates misleading attitudes. In nature such opposites are not alternatives, but similitudes. An image needs be found that caters for such a case. The long-established concept of form and content can serve such a purpose.§ Because of its history the concept has many interpretations (see Chapter 4) but in simple terms it is this. Form is that which encompasses the limits of the concept, its shape being formed by its conterminous contact with its surrounding reality. The form holds within itself the content – those essential ingredients that maintain the form – therefore the form can be said to be finite, while the content is infinite. When discussing material objects, like a stone, the surrounding reality is easy to recognise and identify; when abstract – like an idea – its contacting reality is not so simple to identify. When considering a concept like a sport personality, this too is difficult. It can of course be simply nominalistic with no particular meaning, but if there is a specific meaning it will need to relate to the whole person. For example, it will have to refer to the relationship with the community in which the individual has been nurtured; so to get to the understanding of personality, it can be said to have form and content. The form is that recognised and identified by the surrounding groups, the content is made up of characteristics provided by the individual.

What follows is an attempt to outline some of these characteristics. There are so many that only general explications will be made, otherwise there would have to be so many exceptions that it could be confusing. With luck, however, there will be enough to make the point – that there is more to tactics than just linking one attack with another. I tend to accept that there is such a thing as a sport personality, which can mean that top sportsmen – but I had better confine the discussion to judo – top judo-men are not the same as good judo-men. They are different sorts of people. That does not mean better, but different. There is a growing conviction among some researchers that even physiologically there could be great differences, and certainly psychological differences have always been recognised. Motivation to participate, for example, can be fundamentally different (more about that later) and that would definitely affect the degree of application. So what are they like, these top judo performers? From the limited research that has been done the following is a thumb-nail sketch of such a performer.*

This top judo performer will be very conservative, reluctant to change his ways, ready to conform to generally accepted modes of behaviour. He tends to lack confidence and is unsure of himself; he prefers living within himself and finds mixing with people difficult. He is a pacifist and does not like violence, but is very physically orientated; that is, physical values (e.g. movement articulation, efficient action) are important to him and play a large part in his life-assessment. He will be much influenced by strong personalities, but have little ability to judge whether the strength is for good or bad. Creativity and imagination are in short supply but to compensate there will be tenacity and application. Culture is low on his list of priorities, although he likes being 'comfortable'. He is steadfast and has a utilitarian attitude to life.

In the propaganda literature of judo it is frequently claimed that judo training gives confidence and is cathartic for 'bad' tendencies, e.g. bullying of one kind or another. It is a grossly exaggerated claim. The 'confidence' gained (to make up for their natural timidity) is too

---

* Compared to the research done on male sportsmen there is very little on women. For various practical reasons I included no women in my own research, so I have no direct research experience of female attitudes to top performance. When trying to correlate some of the existing results there does appear to be a difference in attitude profile, but its magnitude – at the present – is not apparent.

often brashness and a bullying tendency is as often encouraged (and made worse) as it is suppressed. Judo training, like any training, will only react with whatever is there. If an individual brings a 'deviant' attitude to judo it will probably be made more deviant; if there is a socially generous nature there that too could be made more so.

To complicate things further, activities or sports are of themselves very extroverted and ostentatious. The skills have to be exhibited before many spectators where the competitor's personality is on full display. Those spectators will expect him to be violent, gaudy and super-confident, in short almost everything opposite to what is really inside him: therefore if he wants to succeed in the sport the aspiring judo champion may need to wear the cloak of all these characteristics; he may well find himself having to act the part of an extroverted, ostentatious exhibitionist. If he is spiritually strong enough he could well enjoy the performance (like many other professional actors), but if there is an inner weakness, such a schizophrenic existence can cause mental bewilderment as to which one of these people he really is. In extreme cases it could cause psychiatric illness.§ This role-playing is a very important part of top sport performance and individuals can become so clever at it that often it becomes difficult for the coach to distinguish the 'real' from the 'pretend' self.* However, if the coach is to build this factor of personality into an individual's tactical plan (which he must do) then he will need to try and diagnose the person – without letting his own expectations/prejudices be imposed on the trainee.

Having analysed the personality, the psychological characteristics, the simpler job of assessing the physical characteristics must be undertaken: items like body flexibility, motor educability, appreciation and utilisation of space – both in terms of space within the fighting area and space around the two bodies, i.e. can the individual twist and turn in the air, does he have a gymnastic facility? Is there a large or a small movement vocabulary?§ Is there a sense of rhythm (very good judo performers are often good dancers)? Is the quality of movement refined or gross? Is there good or poor control over body function? To use the concept of Teilhard de Chardin, what is the degree of consciousness within the individual's noosphere?§

---

* In the short story *The Lion's Skin*, Somerset Maugham makes the valid point that if the pretend self is lived full-time, it eventually becomes the real self, whilst the original real self dies. It raises the intriguing query: what distinguishes real reality from pretend reality?

The coach, and the individual concerned, must of course appreciate that there are no preferential physical characteristics for a top judo performer. When I started judo many years ago it was inferred and even said on occasions that to get to the top of the judo skill mountain, the individual had to be flexible. This is of course spurious. It is the job of the good coach, or the more independent perspicacious performer, to modify the skills to fit the physical characteristics. If there are some deficiencies (e.g. lack of power, slowness of response) they must be compensated by developing other strengths. The individual need not despair if his physical profile does not match up with some mythical skill template. The skill form is finite, but the content infinite. It should be the primary function of *kata* (structured) training to emphasise this very point.

For example, the *nage-no-kata* (selected throwing styles), as its title implies, is to do with the structuring of throwing form. That form is decided by the criteria selected by the person who compiled it, the content (position of hands, feet etc.) is the business of the people who perform it. It must vary to suit the many different people who wish to participate in and learn from *kata* training. The coach then has to decide to what degree or extent does the trainee want to understand exactly what he is supposed to be doing. Educational theorists will try and make the point that it is 'better' if the individual has the training rationale explained to him, for that makes him more aware and therefore it is more 'educational'.§ But pragmatic coaches know there are many top performers who do not want to know why they do 'it', they just want to *do*. The misunderstanding that creeps in here is that the theorists get carried away by their own enthusiasm for learning. They insist on seeing awareness/understanding as a sequential process. First one stage is explained and explored, then another, then another, till the 'steps' of understanding lead to comprehension of the whole.§ Some people do improve comprehension in this way, but others prefer other ways. A reason for the individual taking up sport is because he has an affinity with certain of its intrinsic qualities – the expression of particular mental processes in particular physical forms. Such preferences do not need to be sequential. To use a power analogy, it is like an electric circuit, functions can be wired up in series or parallel. An artist like Raphael with his omnicompetence in structure as well as in form does not have to create his originality on the basis of some sequential, developmental process.§ He could have had an appreciation of finality, of completeness (but not of the 'whole') before he ever began. The Gestaltists were of course trying to point to something of this kind when they opined that *Gestalt* was the 'whole', the totality, but I have always felt they did not go far enough.§ Critics of that conceptual approach said, rightly in my view, that although the *Gestalt* did offer a focus of attention, Gestaltists had not considered the background. That can be as important as the *Gestalt* itself, but in a different scale of function.§ Those people who rise above hypothesis appear to have that ability to 'see' function at all levels and in all manner of ways, *at the same time.** This synchronisation of understanding and confrontation, independent of sequence or categorisation, is what gives insight to the genius.§

Sport performers, even at top level, may not have this level of comprehension, but they could have a scaled-down version. They can, for example, approach the business of improving performance from a very existential standpoint. For them skill is a function of being. Sartre made much sense when he replaced the tag 'motivation' with that of 'intention'. His justification was that motivation was not a cause, but then he added a touch of piquancy by saying that although intention could be a cause, it could also be empty of determinism.§ This is an attitude found frequently in Zen Buddhism, when it tries to deal with the ephemerality of skill.§ Ambiguous phrases like 'do without doing', 'think without thinking', 'the unity of the duality'** abound in the literature and are but feeble attempts to avoid getting involved in what seems to be an ubiquitous demand for 'sequential logic' and therefore 'sequential education'. To insist as some educationalists do that sequential learning is the most desirable, can be not only misleading but time-wasting. If the individual is not a 'sequential type', sequential rationalisation will benefit him but little.§ Certainly when I was trained I was given very little (if any) explanation as to why I was doing/learning something, but the 'pointless' exercises contained well-thought-out constructive 'time bomb' qualities, that tended to 'explode' into flashes of illumination much

---

* To many, here was the enigma of Bernard Shaw: he would juxtapose the apparently sublime and equally apparently trivial and treat them as the same. As Eliza in *Pygmalion* says to Professor Higgins: 'Colonel Pickering treats a flower girl as if she was a duchess'; and Higgins' retort is: 'I treat a duchess as if she was a flower girl.'

** When training in *aiki jitsu* under Professor Tomiki he often used the symbol of prayer, the placing of two hands together as signifying the purpose of prayer and religion – the duality of God and man, the yin and yang becoming one.

later, at times when understanding was made essential by pressure of actual circumstances.

Having said that, in what may appear to be a very complicated manner, it must also be said that some top performers are too dull to understand and therefore do not want any explanation of what they are supposed to be doing. Phrases like 'I want to do judo not talk about it', 'Why should I read a book, I already know what I want to know', 'My coach/teacher has done all the learning for me, why should I do any more', abound in judo circles. In some contexts of course these phrases have complete validity, and are quite acceptable provided that people with such attitudes are not purporting to coach others. There is a verse in the New Testament that says: 'And if the blind lead the blind, they shall both fall into the ditch.'

Having decided if his trainee does want to understand what is going on (assuming the coach himself knows) and to what extent he wants to know, then the coach can begin to build a tactical repertoire for the individual. The scope of such a repertoire will be decided by the needs and skills of the individual as well as his aspirations.

Tactical theory can be gleaned from the massive amount of military literature accumulated over the centuries. Writers like Sun tsu, Julius Caesar, Machiavelli, Sherman, Fuller, Hart, will outline and elaborate upon the many theories on front and flank attacks, attacks by surprise and stealth, attacks by deceit and cunning, by feint and treachery, all needing a place in the judo-man's repertoire.§ Those same writers will describe the purpose of training and how specialist training can be organised. For example, before the battle of Zama Scipio had to plan how he was going to cope with Hannibal's *tokui-waza* (favourite technique), the elephants. The tactics he developed to counter this battle-winning technique made a significant contribution to his ultimate victory. Scipio started the battle second favourite; Hannibal had the skills, the experience, the organisation to win, yet Scipio by using everything he had turned the tables – a useful lesson for any judo fighter to learn.§ It is a pity of course that judo text-books on tactics cannot be quoted, but the truth is that apart from one or two exceptions* judo writers do not write about tactics. It has already been conceded that judo rules of competition do not encourage the development of tactics, but the paucity of information

---

* The notable exception is Peter Barnett.§ His books made a significant contribution to the coaching of tactics. My own book *All About Judo* also contains extensive discussion on the subject.

on the subject shows a sorry lack of knowledge among the text-book writers.

Military writers also discuss strategy, something else important for judo competitors but not discussed in judo books. Opinions can be found on how to 'peak' armies for specific campaigns, and how officers (coaches?) can be trained to devise tactics for the men under them. Hannibal is always worth studying – the master of getting the most from the little his governing body gave him. His strategy was to bring the superior enemy to him, never staying in the one place long enough for the enemy to get the measure of him. By continually manoeuvring he would split the enemy's forces and then hit hard the fragmented parts. The tactics of the battle of Cannae are useful for the judo-man to note – the heavy frontal attack, the retreat from the counter-attack, the enclosing of the enemy with his fast wings! With practice the imaginative coach can easily translate these tactics into judo. The heavy frontal attack is something like *taiotoshi*; the opponent counters by surging forward, trying to swamp the attack with power. By moving quickly to the flanks the counter-counter-attack comes from the flanks, throws like *ashiguruma, hiza guruma*.

Looking at the strategies of generals like Ghengis Khan and Napoleon, it is interesting to see that they made the innovation of building armies for specific types of known opposition. The complement of the *tumans* (Ghengis's strategic armies) was varied, the number of cannon in the artillery regiments were altered, partly to fool the enemy, partly to make the logistics of supply easier. Another possible lesson for the fighting judo-man – have a range of skills and tactics (in terms of power, fitness and complexity) so that changes can be made to suit the strength of the opposition, the time of the year and the venue, and keep the opposition guessing as to what are the main skills.

Perhaps before leaving the military scene a mention could be made of that influential writer Karl von Clausewitz and his realistic observation that war is but an extension of politics. War in the past has been an essential part of man's progress. It provided a comprehensive stimulus to mental and physical growth that was second to none. But to fulfil that function there had to be physical participation in battle, a time-scale that allowed for development of technology and a casualty rate that ensured group survival. War has now changed its nature; it has none of these criteria and therefore no longer serves its historical function. A future war will not be participatory, but long-distance killing. It will be a different type of war and one in which it is to be hoped we shall not be asked to indulge.*

But if there is no war – of the 'old-fashioned' kind – there will still be a need for some stimulating activity. That need will have to be distributed among a range of activities, and sport would be one of the more obvious recipients. But as a possible source of such a cultural stimulus it would also have to accept the other responsibility of old-fashioned war, and be an extension of politics.

Sport has never of course been free of politics, but until now only that type of politics that goes with factious squabbling and sophistry related to such trivialities as the definition of amateurism. With its change in social role, sport has the opportunity to take a mature position among those groups who see it as their duty to influence – wherever possible – political issues. Whether sport is mature enough itself to recognise and accept this responsibility remains to be seen. Hearing the plaintive cries from some quarters in sport, pleading that sport should be apolitical, perhaps it is not, but hopefully as with other art forms sportspeople will grow out of such an isolationist attitude and accept that politics is life and therefore sport must play its part in it.§

Conclusion

The harmonious integration of personality and physical characteristics should go to make up what Napoleon called the 'coup d'oeuil militaire': the ability to glance over a battle layout and assess quickly what must be done and how best to do it. The top judo performer or coach should cultivate the same 'glance', but it will take time, training and a conscientious application to all that which has been outlined in this chapter – and more besides.

---

* The prognostication of Bertrand Russell is recalled here: 'I do not know precisely what the weapons of World War III will be, but I do know those of World War IV – sticks and stones!'

Chapter 2
Countering Skills

'In the Donnunblitzen Stadium 50,000 Euro-citizens roared themselves into a state of explosive excitement. It was the first of those matches that would decide who received the medals. Bloomwitz had the whole of La Belle France behind him and all the skills that money could buy. Hardcastle was a product of the British squad system and knew that if he could stay on his feet for the duration of this match he could earn himself big boodle. The battle began. The spectators yelled themselves into action, breaking blood vessels to make the name of their hero heard above the clamorous din. Each man had previously won the title, so knew the game and would give the crowd something to remember. Hardcastle was apprehensive; Bloomwitz cautious. One small mistake, a loss of three points and the glory was down the drain. Any error of judgement would be met with a successful counter! The situation demanded a wary, defensive approach. A precipitous move was dangerous, but so was too much delay. A solid defence met a solid defence. It settled down into a war of attrition. Who would make the first mistake? The crowd's enthusiasm dwindled too – the match that should have been dynamite was merely boring . . .'

That is the beginning of an imaginary report of a top judo match and the role usually given to countering skills – salvaging an already lost position. The attitude found in most extant training systems, à propos of countering, is to let the other man attack first and then – if luck holds – turn the tables on him by using a countering technique. Such an attitude does have a certain degree of validity but it is a very limited interpretation of countering and therefore has various negative spin-offs which are best avoided.

Here are some of them:

1. It develops a very negative understanding of counters, i.e. that they can only be done *after* the opponent has done something.
2. It allows the opponent to have and keep the initiative, in terms of when to attack (a great psychological advantage).
3. To allow a skilful player to *start* an attack may give him too much of an advantage when it comes to trying to stop him (and he cannot often then be stopped).
4. It accepts that the opponent is the better man – again a psychological advantage that should not be lightly given.

So the purpose of this chapter is to see countering not as a defensive action but as an attacking one. Countering is a part of an attacking sequence, not the desperate last-ditch stand of a fighter who has lost the match before it has begun. If the purposes of countering skills are laid out, it is recognisable that defensive-countering *is* a part of the total countering scene, but only a small part of it.

What are some of those other uses?

1. *The threat.* The opponent is forced to move as a response to a threatened attack; a threat is made (but with no attacking movement), the opponent moves in order to avoid what he thinks is a particular type of attack and that move is countered by a real attack.
2. *The trap.* The competitor exposes what appears to be a weakness in his defence; the opponent recognises and responds to that implied weakness by a direct attack; that attack is countered.
3. *The feint.* An attack is actually launched, but is controlled in terms of commitment and objective. The opponent moves defensively against such an attack; the counter-move is countered by a full-scale direct attack.
4. *The traditional.* The competitor launches a sudden, unexpected attack, the opponent has to respond spontaneously to that attack by trying to exploit its power for his own countering skills. There are two subdivisions that need to be recognised:
    (a) countering early; the counter is made immediately after (or before) the attack is launched; control should be good, score should be high – 7 or 10;
    (b) countering late; the attack has been largely successful; the defender is on his way to the ground; control will probably be poor. Score probably low – 3 or 5.

Viewing countering skills from this much broader base allows the coach to train more individuals to take advantage of this aspect of contest-winning, for it should be appreciated that the traditional method of countering, because of its limited form, attracts very few competitors. It is the strong negative aspect of traditional counters that aggressive fighters do not like. Presenting counters as a positive and offensive way of attacking is bound to attract more performers. The style of any attack, be it offensive or defensive, is a projection or extension of an individual's personality or thinking style.§ There will be a pattern of behaviour that can be easily recognised: attack/parry/counter-attack, attack/fail/attack, be-attacked/avoid/counter-attack, and so on. Those patterns will be found in both physical and mental performances of the individual. If the coach wants to teach counter-skills to the individual, he will need to learn what these patterns are and exploit them accordingly. To try to cut across such patterns would be time-wasting and destructive of other existing skills. For example, to try to coach a technique that is 'be-attacked/avoid/counter-attack' to a man with a natural pattern of 'attack/fail/attack' would be doomed to frustration and exasperation.

Learning countering skills

If there is a propensity to counter-attack in a certain private way, be it in judo or life, in deed or word, then that talent must be exploited. A talent is a matured propensity; if it is rich and full, little explanation may need to be given about how things are done, because the acquisition of skills is its own justification. If there is little initial talent available, the lack will need be made up by perseverance from the performer and wisdom from the coach.* By the same token, when there is much talent, not every learning stage need be passed through. Many short cuts can be taken (perhaps going straight to the final form of the skill). If talent is short, perhaps many forms of structured training sessions need to be designed and experienced.§

---

§ When this mark is found, it means that there is a 'further reading' section in the bibliography.

* There are many historical examples of men who got to the top of their vocation in spite of what appeared to be a poor talent at the outset; Cicero, Gauguin and Somerset Maugham, for instance.

Threat and counter

Given a reasonable amount of competitive experience, say brown belt or above, or ten/twelve months' training, most conscientious trainees will kinesthetically understand that there are only a few basic types of attack – to wit, three:

1. The attack will come at him from head on, straight from the front. Techniques like *uchimata*, *seoinage*, and some *sutemi-waza* will be assumed capable of crashing through any defence offered and of scoring high points, 7 or 10. It is seldom true. Unless there is a significant disparity in skill levels such primitive attacks, with no preparation, are seldom successful and what is more are easily countered.
2. Much the same thing – the attack will come from dead ahead, but instead of trying to throw the target forward, it will throw him backwards. There is no subtlety in this kind of attack. It bears a strong resemblance in principle to the infantry advances in the First World War; because there is bravery, resolution and intent involved in the attack, somehow it is assumed it will overcome massed machine guns or defensive arm actions. The war attacks did not succeed, nor do unprepared *ouchi* or *kouchi* attacks. The defences are too strong; they must be weakened first by diversionary raids.
3. The attack comes from the side. This is a more subtle approach (one therefore seldom used by judo competitors). Instead of charging straight at the opponent the attacker first moves to the side and starts from there. Modified techniques like *ashiguruma*, *oguruma*, *kosoto* and *osoto* are typical of this kind of attack. Moreover, these attacks are not so easy to stop, firstly because they are unexpected (not from the front) and secondly because they avoid the main line of defence, the straight arms. If the 'underdog' is fully aware of these general attacking forms he may be able to utilise this knowledge successfully against his stronger opponent. If he can persuade the hit-man that he is just an ordinary player with inferior skills, he may be able to open a gap in the hit-man's superiority. Let us look at some threat/counter-attacks.

The threat/counter-attack

The target threatens with a straight-back throw, say *ouchi*; he purposely lets his left grip go soft (although it does not let go) but tightens up the right (collar) hand. The hit-man feels the tightening of the right hand and assumes the attack-direction will be towards his own left-back corner. Quite quickly, because he only has to move his hips an inch or two, he adjusts his weight, putting most of it on his right foot, so allowing the left leg to swing free if it is hooked by an *ouchi* attack. It is the kind of subtle response the target has hoped for; as he feels the hips move he adjusts his own weight by pulling his right hip back, as this allows his right foot to be weightless and capable of moving anywhere. It goes forward near the opponent's right foot and the left foot drops back; there is no time to change the hand pressure so they are left as they were. The right leg swings up into *oguruma*, completed by the target rolling completely over the top of the hit-man.

A different situation: the target moves quickly to the (hit-man's) left flank. From there he threatens with an *osoto* or an *ashiguruma*. The hit-man guesses the final action and gently moves his left hip forward (closing up the gap between the bodies) and stiffening the left leg, thus allowing the right leg to be capable of moving freely. If the attack was any more than a threat, and the target's right leg lifted off the ground for any reason, the hit-man's counter would be fast and most effective. However, the target has no intention of doing that, instead when he feels the left hip move that inch or so forward, he attacks with *taiotoshi* against the hit-man's hard left leg. Normally the opponent in this position attacked by a normal *taiotoshi* (one aimed against his *right* leg or his hips), would be able to step round it easily enough. Now, because the throwing action is against his fixed *left* leg (knocking it backwards, out from underneath him), it is not easy to step over.* Such an attack is feasible if the hit-man is better than the target and is capable of appreciating what could be happening, but assesses it wrongly.

Another purpose of the threat/counter-attack is to change the opposition's posture and give the weaker competitor a chance to attack aggressively – with some hope of success. The hit-man is standing quite straight, moving around quickly and tightly – knowing his

---

* Another excellent example of the possible range of a throwing skill. What coach would *teach* a *taiotoshi* that attacks the *left* leg of an opponent? Yet it is done frequently enough by experienced performers. Notice the occasion when, in defence, the opponent pulls his *right* side back to block/stop *taiotoshi*; it then (accidentally) makes the strong left leg the weak link.

superiority. The target threatens with a front attack, probably something like *tsurikomigoshi*. The experienced hit-man knows that such an attack should result in a lowering of the centre of gravity (some form of crouch), so he does the opposite and straightens his posture more, lifting forward onto his toes so that he can move fast and possibly use a counter. The target is hoping for this kind of double-bluff and is ready to use a special attack – should he get the response. He does! The target's 'counter' attack is an *osoto* with the right leg sweeping very high, taking the hit-man's buttocks – and legs – out from under him. The very high sweep negates any chance the hit-man has of moving his legs quickly as he had hoped to do, to make a counter-attack. The very high leg sweep also allows the target to adopt an unusual throwing movement, very different from the 'standard' pattern (i.e. 'standard' is curved forward; 'unusual' is straight). This makes it a good example of a technique being modified drastically to become a skill for a special circumstance – as with Napoleon.

A by the way

No doubt some of the more experienced readers will complain that what I have described above are linked attacks or combinations, not counters. In a sense their complaint is justified; such a skill can be classed as *renraku-waza*, but more importantly it should show how difficult it is to differentiate the two in practice. When a competitor makes a consciously defensive movement, in order to stop or prevent an attack being made – either real or assumed – does not the other competitor *counter* that move when he uses it to complete a different attack? The Japanese have a name for it: *go-no-sen jitsu*.

The coach will have to decide which way he will put it to the trainee, when he is coaching it. The major criterion will be the personality of the recipient. If, for example, the threat of *kouchi* was used with the reality of *taiotoshi*, the audience would see just one movement, *taiotoshi*; only the participants would know that the attacker had forced a response by a threat. Now perhaps the competitor likes 'showing off' to the spectators, in which case such an attack would not suit him, for he would want his fans to see him make that first attack. Therefore the coach would not waste time teaching him the threat/counter-attack.

The trap/counter-attack

This is the obverse side of the threat/counter-ploy. It takes courage, confidence and experience. The principle is that the attacker surreptitiously allows a weakness to appear in his defence. It can take the form of a shoulder being allowed to slope an inch or two too far forward or back, a foot to be just that little bit too far to the side, front or back, the head to be ever so slightly tilted too far left or right. The opponent, feeling the weakness, attacks. The ambusher, knowing it is coming, counters fast and effectively. Courage is needed to expose the weakness; confidence is needed to ensure the weakness is adequately exposed, but not enough to give away a terminal ten; experience is needed to know what kind of attack the opponent will use against that particular offered opportunity.

An example: if the right shoulder is allowed to creep just a little too far forward, the opponent will see *ippon-seoinage* as the most suitable form of attack, and use it. The sagacious one knows the hit-man can do *ippon-seoi* (he has watched him fighting other people often enough) so he is confident that if the hit-man accepts the bait he will try *ippon-seoi*. He does. The attack is immediately destroyed by the *seoi*-man being dragged over backwards and pinned by some form of *yoko-shihogatame*.

In ground-grappling (*ne-waza*) one competitor is on top of the other, but both are struggling for a winning position. The man underneath allows an arm to get just that little too far from his body. With great satisfaction the hit-man snatches it and goes for *juji-gatame*. As he rolls back, thinking he is in the process of applying the lock, the target leaps forward and not only gets out from underneath (never a good position) but actually counter-attacks with a side-pin (*yoko-shihogatame*).

A by the way

Emerging from the discussion on countering is a long-argued problem which concerns the performer himself and his coach. Should the trainee stay within his talents or should he go outside them? There are strong arguments for both sides.§ Those who suggest that training should stay within the constraints of the talent argue that because the effectiveness of the skill has a 'flying start' on account of its very innateness, so it is only sensible to cultivate that range of skill and make it as good as possible. Certainly it must be conceded that the 'flying start' plus a knowledgeable nurturing can produce a tremendous level of effectiveness. Others, on the contrary, suggest that concentration on just the inherited ability will stultify general development and make it easy for the opposition to recognise and nullify that singular ability.

As always if two alternatives are presented as if a choice has to be made – one or the other – I tend to say 'neither – but both'. There is more at stake here than just selecting which is the best way to use a skill talent. How is any talent to be exploited? The way chosen will help to shape a life-style. There are many factors involved. Take one that is common in social discussion, boredom. Boredom is a major hazard in any training plan. Learning, whatever form it takes, is essentially repetitive, which is potentially boring. Sportsmen by dint of their propensity for sport are prepared to accept a great deal of repetition and the boredom that goes with it, but there is a limit. Thresholds of boredom vary from individual to individual; deciding factors will be items like intelligence and curiosity. Those who are both curious and intelligent will seldom be bored by their environment, those who are neither will invariably be so. The coach would need to recognise the individual's levels of tolerance and know when and how to avoid them. Some performers will need 'standard' skill practices greatly simplified in order to avoid boredom (a matter of not overtaxing their capacities); others will need the same practices made much more complicated in order to provide a challenge. Some will see judo as physical chess, others as nothing more than a tit-for-tat, hammer and slam – the last man standing up is a sissy.

Champions as well as good citizens will come equally from both extremes; but too much hammer and slam and society may well lose a good citizen. Early victories (in their careers) will no doubt be achieved by those skills that come easily to the aspiring champion. Thanks to his talent he no doubt learnt them with little effort and because of that facility has not bothered to discover why they work or even how he uses them. Because the skills are essentially simplistic – indeed the word primitive could be used – their effectiveness will not be long-lasting. Because of the nature of these skills and the lack of understanding, they will soon disintegrate under the ever-increasing stress of continuous top competition. It is at this stage that the man who wants to become king must go beyond his natural range of talent and cultivate more complex skills.§ It takes courage, dedicated aspiration and a good coach. The painter Raphael was an inspiring example of a man who learnt much from his coaches Michelangelo and Leonardo, and kept on raising his skill level when others had thought he had gone as far as he could.§.

The feint-attack/counter-attack

This is an extension of the threat/counter-attack; in this case an actual part-attack is made (the feint), the opponent responds to this real attack and that response is countered. The whole situation is of a much lower skill order than the threat/counter (just to give some indication, the feint/counter is about 1 or 2 dan level, while the threat/counter is about 4 or 5 dan standard). The less-skilled opponent has not the experience to recognise mere threats, he needs gross movements to show that he is being attacked. However, the feint-attack, although having of necessity many of the marks of an intended-scoring attack (or the opponent would not respond), lacks certain factors. The major differences would be the retention of body-weight by the attacker; in practice that means keeping the hips back out of any forward movement, then feet would not be taken very close to the opponent (so preventing the opponent from kicking them either in attack or defence); both feet would – wherever possible – be kept in contact with the ground (maximum stability). Hands would initially make jerking actions on the opponent's jacket but once the feint started would quickly subside into non-action.

Some examples

An energetic form of *harai-tsurikomi-ashi* is made, the hit-man feverishly avoids the scything swipe of the right foot, steps or even jumps backwards (only about 4-6 inches, 10-15 cm). The target, having the weight and movement under full control, plants the right foot on the gound (near the opponent), swings the left foot back into the full-attack position and goes for *uchimata*.

In a similar vein an *uchimata* is used as the feint-attack. The target pivots on the spot, making a half-turn (he does not move any closer to the opponent). The target's right leg is swung back in a deliberate, rather slow manner. There is no weight commitment. Again the hit-man does not want to be in the same bit of space as the swinging leg, so he moves aside to his right (possibly hoping to make a counter-attack of his own). In doing so he turns very much sideways. The target's right foot is quickly put to the ground and *harai-tsurikomi-ashi* is used against the hit-man's right foot/leg.

In competition here is the start of what can be a whole rally of attacks, defences and counters. The very simple counters mentioned above could pivot on the use of *uchimata*. If the *uchimata* is used as a high-scoring attack, it may set off one lot of responses in the opponent; if used as a low-scoring attack or feint, it may elicit a whole different set of responses with definite results.

A by the way

Some writers on judo techniques advocate that feint-attacks should be done with the intention of making a high score (full commitment). They rationalise it by saying that only with such commitment could the attack carry sufficient intention of purpose to make the other man respond.* I have never gone along with this view. If there is full commitment and the opponent does avoid the line of attack, I would suggest the attacker is in no position to change his line of attack. It would be like Hannibal's elephant charge in the opening round of the Battle of Zama, when carried away by their own momentum the elephants exposed the flanks of the Carthaginian cavalry which were promptly attacked by the Romans.§ It was the first of a series of 'overshoots' on the part of Hannibal, which eventually cost him the battle.

The traditional counter

In orthodox judo teaching it is usually assumed that a competitor, against the same level of expertise, can make an attack which is totally unexpected and unheralded, yet at the same time there is sufficient 'looseness' in the attack for the surprised opponent to rally his resources and inject a countering force into the attacking movement before it is completed, and with such effectiveness that it completely turns the tables and makes it he who scores terminal 10. In practice there is seldom a time when such an unsuspected attack is launched (it could be questioned whether it ever happens). As long as the two fighters are somewhere near each other's ability there is invariably some small sign that an attack is on the way; a change in rhythm, a peculiar movement of the head, a twitch of the hips, a change in body tension. With such warning 'clues' the defender can take defensive/countering actions. If the attack is launched with really no warning the only thing that will stop a terminal score is the attacker's own inefficiency. Another possible exception, and this will only happen if there is a big discrepancy in skill level, is when the superior performer underestimates his opposition and launches an unsuspected but careless attack. The alert opponent would then have a chance to organise a counter.

---

* The Japanese adage used to support this contention is that the lion uses the same powerful blow to kill the rabbit as the deer. I wonder! It seems an unnecessary and very uneconomical use of strength.

Some examples
Countering early

The hit-man launches a very strong *ouchi* attack. It is unexpected and the left leg is driving strongly in the right direction and the right leg is hooked hard in behind the opponent's left leg; everything appears good for a high score. Now, carelessly, the hit-man allows his chin to lift slightly, which moves the hips a couple of inches too far forward. It is enough. The target, using his trapped left leg as a pivot, turns back hard towards his left, exploiting the arch in the attacker's back to swing him sideways and onto his back – for a good score.

Another instance. The attack is *uchimata*. The move into the throwing position is fast and dynamic. The right hip is where it should be (against the target's left hip), the hands pull down and round. Good! However, the left foot is too much under the hip area (preventing weight commitment), it hits the ground between the opponent's feet. In that instant the target feels the lack of drive and immediately throws himself into a turning move to his left, swinging his left foot forward hoping to make contact with the attacker's leg. (If he does, the record books will call it *kosoto-gaeshi*.) He does and it is a good score.

A by the way

In days of yore a phrase frequently found in judo teaching was 'how to break balance'. It was suggested that before any throw could be attempted, the opponent's balance had to be broken.§ In practice it is difficult to ascertain what this meant, although in theory it was simple enough. By subtle pulling on a partner's jacket, it was said, he is 'tilted' forward onto a point on the edge of his feet/base, i.e. toes. Arabesquely poised on this small contact point with mother-earth, he was said to be vulnerable to any throwing attack. (It is yet another intriguing enigma of the 'old school' in judo; why was 'balance breaking' never mentioned in *ne-waza*?) Modern tradition seems to assume that if a man is ever reduced to this ridiculous position, there is nothing he can do – not even move. He simply waits till that sword of Damocles splits him in two. It is not true, of course. However precariously the individual is perched on one toe he can certainly move and what is more if he is thrown from this position he is quite capable of turning and twisting in the air as he falls. Presumably what the 'old school' was trying to say is that the manoeuvring of an opponent into a circumstance where he loses control over his movements is important if an attack is to succeed. Whether that is brought about by shocking him into immobility by use of the famous/infamous *kiai* yell, or a smart kick on the shins, or by so confusing his mental processes that he cannot co-ordinate a positive response to an attack, does not really matter.

If this change in conceptualisation is made, from 'break balance' to 'lose control', it not only increases considerably the ways of making the opponent lose control, but also allows the introduction of a whole new range of skills – how to fall/be thrown without losing points.

Some examples
Countering late

The attack is a strong *osoto* from the flank. Everything is good but the right hand; the hit-man's left foot is well to the target's left side, the right leg is hooking up and back, but the right hand has been allowed to go soft (in terms of grip). The throw works. The target's right foot comes off the floor, but he turns on his left foot and begins to rotate backwards; as he does so the slack on his left collar allows him to pull the left shoulder back and twist as he rotates. The target now pulls in with his left hand and pushes hard with his right. The hit-man suddenly finds himself rotating over his own right leg. Of course the target has lost his balance, but not his control, so although he falls over, the twist gets the hit-man onto the ground first and *underneath* the target. A good score.

The attack is *seoinage*. Again all is good and the target is thrown, but the target has managed to get his right shoulder back an inch or two which gives him enough space around the shoulder-girdles to move in. Instead of letting the dip of his shoulders take him over the attacker's right shoulder he twists in the air so that he falls over the attacker's left shoulder. With dexterity he lands on his feet, pushes the attacker over and goes for some evident pin.

A by the way

At the beginning of the chapter mention was made of the idea that the ability to counter was more a matter of mental processes than acquired physical skills. That is, there are certain propensities within a personality that prefer a particular pattern of response to a situation rather than another.*§

An intriguing extension of this counter-type performance is this – are there propensities in personalities for other skills? It is a very controversial subject and much 'heat' is radiated by protagonists of both sides of the argument. Possibly the two most vociferous protagonists within the debate at the moment are Chomsky for innateism and Piaget for constructivism.§ Chomsky's views are the result of his research on the origins of language, while Piaget rests his arguments on his study of children in different learning situations. Ranked along with these two, on the respective sides, are many people with equal status and prestige who argue just as strongly for each respective hypothesis. For of course in the end that is all it is, a hypothesis; but the man who is a coach must choose one bias or the other because it will affect the way he teaches and coaches. The fact that there is such a split among the specialists on the subject will not make his task of deciding an easy one. A lot of reading and cogitation will be needed to help clarify the issues before a stand can be taken.

As always when there is an antinomic 'either/or' proffered the solution is not to choose one at the cost of the other, but take both! Of course the environment is important in any skill-acquiring situation; it cannot be ignored and whenever feasible it must be manipulated in every way possible to stimulate the right kind of skill development, but I for one am of the opinion that there are innate propensities for skills and for quite specific skills at that. In my research, for example, there were a number of indications that give support to this opinion.§ For example, most of the sample in my research had little, if any, justification for dedicating themselves so totally to a specific skill. Most did not know why they started, why they kept training, or what they wanted out of success when they got it. Yet in spite of that nebulosity of purpose (which in the eyes of an educationalist would provide no motivation whatsoever for achieving) they had become champions. Perhaps it is only an illustration of Sartre's existentialism; to achieve success with apparently no determinism would point to the possibility that pure commitment is part and parcel of a propensity – a need – to do a skill well.

Another intriguing conundrum related to this speculation that

---

* It can also work the other way. By studying how a skilful judo-man uses his competitive skill, an assessment can be made of how he will perform in general life situations.

champions are born not made is, to what extent do aspiring champions – unconsciously – exploit those nearest them for their own ends? Do children, who seemingly know nothing about the doing of judo, somehow – in some mysterious way – make their parents take them along to a judo club so that they can join it and become champions?§ Many top performers after investigation are found to have been taken to their sports by a parent or friend when they were quite young.§ They seemed to have had no interest in the sport at the time (and for some time after). They were not aware that they had any particular liking for the sport. It was not their idea to start the sport, yet having started it they found it 'easy' to do. (Here 'easy' means that the fundamentals were quickly mastered and an understanding of what was needed grew with little cultivation.) So in spite of an apparent indifference to the purpose and objectives of the game, they seemed to have discovered an affinity to the skill that survived that indifference.

If the top performer is a different person from the one who only plays at the lowest level for enjoyment (and never gets past that stage), as I think he is, then different training and learning systems will be needed for the different kinds of participation. Just as the coach cannot expect the same teaching methodology to suit all of his novices equally, for their aspirations will be different, so similarly he should not expect the top performer to learn in the same way as the giftless player. It is for that reason that he should present the whole concept of countering skills in different ways to different people at different levels.

Conclusion

Both the coach and the performer will need to give a lot of thinking time as well as training time to understanding what countering skills are all about – what is the scope of their performance, and how they are best learnt. Certainly they should not simply be considered as a negative skill – the stopping, prevention or destroying of other people's attacks. They should be, and are, positive attacking skills, but applied indirectly as compared to the direct attacks of throwing and grappling skills. The learning of them should add a great batch of skills to the repertoire of competitive tactics.

Chapter 3
Let's Start Again

'The Executive Council had watched many judo competitions. The members reluctantly, although never in public, admitted that on the whole the experience was a boring one. But then there was nothing they could do about it. It reminded them too much of the fictitious complaint about the 9.15. train from Dublin, whose last carriage always rattled abominably. The railway authorities accepted the complaint and promptly removed the last carriage. The Council cleverly decided to ban all those aspects of contests that could possibly be boring, but did nothing about the teaching of boring judo, which continued to flourish.'

Having finished the last chapter by saying that the teaching methodology should be varied to suit best the person who is learning, perhaps now is the time to talk about ways of launching people into the whole process of acquiring the skills of judo.

It is more than an adage, it is a truism, accepted by many writers on skill, that the first things learnt during the acquisition of a skill will not only stick with the individual until the end of time but will be regurgitated whenever stress-pressure rips away any more lately acquired skill factors.§ The novice who has been traditionally taught during his first few lessons knows that whenever he falls over he must whack the ground with his arm and will therefore whack his arm in a European championship several years later, when the tensions of the occasion have blotted out all his more recently acquired tactical skills. It is very important therefore to give much consideration to

---

§ When this mark is found, it means that there is a 'further reading' section in the bibliography.

what is presented and taught to novices during those initial lessons.

Those who are responsible for the design and instruction of such introductory courses must first decide what are the purposes and objectives. Is it to provide a base for competitive training, an activity for the social player, a game for the children, a physical education for everyone? Whatever the decision it should affect the form and content of the course.§

Let us look at some past examples. In the past not nearly enough thought has been given to what an introductory course is for, therefore it has tended to take on a very strange pattern and has contained very little that was designed to give the novice an understanding of what his particular type of judo should be like. Very similar to the definition of a camel as described in business organisation – a horse designed by a committee – so in the case of a beginners' judo course, a hobby-horse designed by a 'committee' of instructors. It has no mention of scoring, tactics, movement quality, no mention of skills (only techniques), no allowance for individual mental or physical idiosyncrasies. The course, however, contains a plethora of safety measures to the point of neuroticism, repetition of movements that have no contact with competitive reality and a supply of negative attitudes so abundant that it would have stunned Dr Pangloss.§ No wonder judo competition is dull to watch. The enthusiastic learner has to wait till the course is over before he can discover ways of acquiring effective skills, for he gets no help from the beginners' instructor. If he is not an adventurous man, and most judo-men are not (see p. 33), he will not devise his own experimental ways of uncovering those skills that are innate in himself, he will simply project forward all that depressing stuff he learnt on the beginners' course. He will then either lose all of his innate ability (and judo training often does that) or he will find it months, perhaps years, later when it is almost too late.

If this dreadful circle of events is ever to be stopped, the solution must be to change the content of the beginners' courses, to include all the items that form the basis of a competition range of skill. What follows is an attempt to show that perhaps it could be beneficial to put beginners into different kinds of groups, dependent upon what they want from judo, and make the teaching methodology different for each group. When the tyro joins the judo club he fills in an information form, a section of which is concerned with what he wants from judo; the coach in charge then makes up the different groups from those responses. Below is an outline of three such kinds of course.

A course for competitive judo

The members would probably be mostly on the young side, teenagers and early twenties. The course would be built around scoring in competition.

The first thing they would be told is what are the scores (i.e. 3, 5, 7, 10) and what conditions them (landing on back, side etc.) and they would then be shown what that meant.* They would replicate those positions (by movement) in relation to the score numbers. Subsequent to that all attacks taught, whether in vertical or horizontal grappling, would be related to scoring capability. No value judgement would be made regarding the size of score; a 3 is just as important and skilful in a difficult situation as 10 is in an easier one. Falling methods, although naturally concerned with safety (avoiding injury), would be specifically aimed at reducing scores and regaining attacking initiative. If techniques were taught they would be taught in tactical situations, stressing the skill aspect. Everything in the course would be aimed at improving competitive skills immediately. The individual would be encouraged to produce his own version of the course material. If he cannot do that, then he will at least be provided with a 'set of tools' that will stand him in good stead when he gets into competition.

Some examples

A score of 3 is needed. The novice knows what the result must look like (the opponent landing on his bottom or hip). How does he get there by a throwing action? Take the technique of *taiotoshi* as the way. The definition of a throw is given simply as putting a limb or a part of the body in front or behind the opposition and *pushing* him over it. To score 3 with *taiotoshi* the right leg is quickly 'stabbed' across on the outside of the partner's right leg; there is very little if any body turn, and very little weight-commitment. The hands will 'punch' hard to the right and hopefully the opponent will stumble over the blocking right leg, scoring 3.

Such a short, sharp action cannot be done in a static position (as a controlled technique can), therefore not only should it be taught in a simple tactical situation, it *must* be taught thus. Here is where the

---

* An actual lesson plan is not being laid out here, only the general content. Class rhythm in terms of alternating periods of action and rest, structured or unstructured training and the need or not for such factors as 'warm-up' is left to each individual coach.

'contest edge' effect could be introduced early into the training course. The novice is told what the edge is for and all the hazards that are concerned with it. For example, he must not step over the line; if he does it can lose him the match. Here is the opportunity of scoring 3. If the opponent 'bounces' off the edge line there is a chance for a quick score of 3. A line is set up in the training area, and the pairs take turns in 'bouncing' off the edge with the partner trying for a 'stabbing' score of 3.

Starting off a novices' first session in something of this way not only introduces scoring, tactics and location (within contest area) but brings in the business of falling as a gradually changing process. Stumbling over a foot or leg can be a very gentle way of falling down. The novice can learn by stepping over (the leg), sitting down, then rolling over. As the score of the attacks is increased, so the training for the appropriate different kinds of falling is introduced. This is not the place to go deeply into the training of falling methods. I have done that in previous books and they can be read if such detail is needed.§ However, I will discuss this important matter briefly.

In days of yore falling was treated as the last stage of defeat. The attacker would go crashing in for some technique; if the opponent could not stop the attack he would metaphorically shrug his shoulders (not in reality of course) and prepare himself for landing on his back, whacking the ground with his arm (*ukemi-waza*) and conceding defeat.§ To make this action more effective he would be made to practise this form of defeat for hours and weeks – fall over, whack the ground and stand up a loser. The justification for this rather strange training was that it was 'safe'; it prevented injury when thrown. No doubt to some extent that was true, but it inferred two other things which were not true: that it was the only way of falling down and that it was the only way to fall without being injured. Of course trainees want to minimise the risk of injury when they fall (as does everybody else I presume), but equally they do not want to give scores away for nothing, or lose scores when they do not have to, so other falling methods must be devised which fulfil those competitive criteria as well as the safety ones. As always with situations where training methods are to be modified, the original concept needs to be examined and altered first. That having been done, it is comparatively easy to change the physical manifestation; therefore falling must not be seen as a negative phase of being attacked – the symbol of defeat; it must be seen as a positive phase in the countering-attack skills (see Chapter 2). Defeat is not conceded until the referee yells '*Ippon!*' The man who is thrown can learn to turn and twist in the falling space so that he can reduce the score from 10 to 7 or to nothing, from 5 to 3 or to nothing. Not only has such an action reduced the score (and saved the match) but frequently it is such a surprise to the thrower that he is susceptible to an immediate response attack.* Such twists and turns are of course gymnastic movements and they may well need to be learnt away from the hurly-burly of throwing situations. As soon as there is some facility with them they can be introduced into the throwing situation (see pages 103-135).

As the novice progresses through his introductory course and he begins to learn how to score the higher numbers of 7 and 10, he may want to have some simple guidelines that will help him set up the attack he wants to make. (Others may not, they will know kinesthetically what is for what). Here are some points for consideration:

1. *Weight commitment.* To score a terminal 10 it is usually necessary to put the whole dynamic weight into the direction of the intended throw. As the intent is lowered to score lower points, so that weight commitment will be withdrawn (of course if an intended 10-score attack fails for some reason, it too may only score 3, but that is chance, beyond the control of the individual). A 3-score attack will contain very little weight commitment.
2. *Use of hands.* To score terminal 10 normally the hands will be pulled in close to the attacker, trying to make close contact with the bodies. If possible the opponent's head needs to be lower than the attacker's (whether one or both elbows are up or down will depend upon the technique and the performer). Before the attack starts the hands may be doing all kinds of things, pulling, pushing, in company or apart, trying to make the opponent lose control over his movements. Once the attack starts, however, they will need to get close to the attacker's body so they can *push* the opponent down towards the ground (see Chapter 2).

    As the scoring intent lowers, the hands will not need to be so close to the (attacker's) body. When scoring 3, for example, they could be working almost at arms' length, one pulling, one pushing.
3. *Use of feet/legs.* To score terminal 10 the feet, and particularly the driving leg, have got to be in the right position to drive the

---

* It is quite remarkable how often a man who is thrown bounces straight up and throws the thrower. Very much as in the football match, a team scores and the other team quickly rallies and replies within minutes.

committed body-weight into the direction of the intended throw. For any throw which intends to throw the opponent to his front, the driving foot must be close to the opponent's feet (sometimes even past them). If the attack is to send the opponent backwards, then the driving foot wants to be a long way from him to the front. In short, the driving leg wants to be thrusting into the line of the throw.

Again, as the score is reduced, so the position of the driving foot can change. Usually to score an intentional 3 the attack has got to be very quick; there is not enough time to build up power so the driving foot need hardly move from its original position.

4. *Body contact.* It has already been mentioned that if a high score is intended the bodies will need to be kept in close contact to ensure the maximum transfer of power from the attacker to the opponent. This relationship is of course difficult to achieve (particularly if the opponent is more experienced than the attacker), so in practice it will often happen that the equivalent of chest contact will be done through the defensive stiff arms of the opposition. The bodies can be 'locked' together by the attacker pulling himself hard onto the opponent's stiff arms, so there will be a gap between the bodies but body contact will be made through the arms. However, if this also fails it is futile to strive continually for something which is practically impossible to obtain. It is only sensible in such circumstances to go for low scores. Scores of 3 and 5 can be made with big gaps between the bodies.

5. *Opportunity.* For small scores little opportunity is needed (little will be given if the opponent is better!). So the attacker will have to snatch whatever opportunity he can, a careless step there, a drop of the shoulder here and he will have to go for a quick 'stab' of 3. For a high score, the opportunity will need to be planned (unless the opponent makes a gross mistake). It will involve all those things mentioned in the first two chapters.

Emerging from a judo introductory course that has taught what the scores are and how to get them and how to avoid them, some awareness of how the edge of the contest area can affect the skills he performs, and how to create different opportunities for different types of attack, the novice may be capable of gradually developing a skill that is both exciting and effective. What is more, it may produce competition skills that are exciting to watch.

A by the way

Competition, meaning winning, has an ambivalent position in judo. Even the Japanese seem to have doubts about its role in the overall picture. I remember talking to a manager of a Japanese World Championships judo team, who assured me that judo was not a sport. They have words like *shiai* and *shobu* (competition and contest) much like we do and by and large they claim they train for *shiai* and not *shobu*;§ the inference being that winning in *shiai* is not so important as winning in *shobu*. However, their continued adherence to the 'sudden death' one-throw victory and their almost neurotic reaction when a Japanese loses to a foreigner would appear to belie that inference and suggest that in fact they prefer the dramatic win of *shobu*.

By the time judo has travelled half-way round the world to Britain the confusion seems even more profound. On the one hand judo is acknowledged as being non-competitive (e.g. contest skills are not taught on beginners' courses), on the other hand progress is only accepted when proved in before-the-public contests. Again, grading syllabi are designed to test techniques in isolation from any form of competition, yet the results are supposed to relate to effectiveness in competition (e.g. that's how the coloured belts are won). No wonder participants and spectators are confused by what is going on.

Competition seems to have become synonymous with contest and contest has become the be-all and end-all of all judo training. It is a stultifying viewpoint. In my opinion, it would be so much better if there was judo competition rather than judo contest, meaning that a judo match would not end in one big bang, which can be as much luck as skill. Instead there would be a specified period of time stated and within that period the competitors could show their skills to the full. However, if we must have 'big bang' contests why cannot there also be competition for those who prefer the more challenging on-going skill against skill match? After all, there is that form of competition between dancer and dancer (who can perform the more complicated, exciting, impossible dancing feats), between musician and musician (who can play the faster or the more complicated melodies). Why cannot some judo performers have that kind of competition? – those players who simply want to perform the skills superbly well without the inhibition that if they make one mistake they are finished. This could produce hitherto unknown flights of virtuoso skill.

Judo for the social player

For brevity of treatment I have grouped under this one heading those people who want to 'keep fit by judo', to 'keep thin by judo', who want to acquire judo skills but not take part in formal contests. This wide range of motivation will need a wide range of satisfaction.§

Some examples

To satisfy the 'keep fitter' who will probably be in the late twenties and over it may be better to start with horizontal-grappling. Risk is minimal, because gravity is eliminated and there is plenty of isometric exercise and cardio-vascular stimulation. The worst potential injury is the 'flying elbow' that can crack someone across the nose. Depending on the group's physical competency it may be better to start with a sequence or pattern of linked offensive and defensive moves; or, if they are physically inept, to use single attack and defence moves. Again content is infinite and can be adapted to suit the group.

For those who want skills more than fitness it may be better to start them with vertical-grappling; to stress, from the outset, movement quality and patterns; the techniques are taught as punctuation after the sentences of movement have been learnt. The essence at the beginning of learning is co-operation between the members of the group. They learn to move skilfully through their own efforts and by assessing and advising one another. As they begin to differentiate between speeds of certain movements and they can change direction easily without losing control of their bodies in the change, judo techniques are introduced. The type of technique will depend on those qualities which are being dealt with at any particular time in the programme.

An example

A simple change of direction pattern is taught. The learning pair is Mr A and Mr B. They move in a straight line in the direction that Mr B is facing. After a few steps they change direction obliquely (see diagram) with Mr B still facing the same original way. They move straight, facing one way, they change direction but still facing the same way. The straight line movement is then made fast, the oblique slow. Now they have learnt change of direction and change of pace. When that is done (and it should only take a few minutes) an *ouchi* is 'slotted in' just after the change of direction – done by Mr B. The movement pattern should help Mr B achieve the technique. He is moving to his right side/back; that should help him hook his right leg in (behind Mr A's left leg). The direction of throw is back from whence they have come, so that should give Mr B guidance when he has to control his body into the direction of throw.

What are these movement qualities they should be aware of? Let me try and give some indication:

Slow, heavy movements. Usually contain strengths or power (but not always); they are very controlled and provide thinking time (what to do next).

Fast, light movements. Seldom contain power as a purposeful premeditation, but they can have a ballistic quality which once initiated can be difficult to control. It demands speed of thought and stimulates fast thinking.

The developing judo performer should realise that there is a tremendous interaction between states of mind (thinking) and movement. The mind may need to start the type of movement, i.e. slow, fast, defensive, offensive, but once having done that the body movement will influence the mind as to how it continues to think, i.e. slow movement will make the mind move slowly.* If the judo trainee

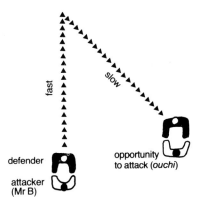

Shows a simple tactical situation for a novice.

---

* One of the hazards of a 'heavy' warm-up, i.e. lots of slow, ponderous movements, is that it can set a very poor mental state for the rest of a training session. Warm-up is as much, if not more, for the mind as for the body.

wants to change the normal relationship, that is body and mind, as he may well have to do (i.e. to think fast when he is moving slowly), it will need much conscientious training.

Dividing movement into just fast and slow is not of course nearly enough. There will be jerky, smooth, what could be called 'double-think' movements (trying to do two things at the same time), cowardly movement and brave movement. In fact the whole personality of the individual will be reflected in the type of movement he uses. Indeed with study and experience some personality characteristics can be assessed through the movement quality. It is this relationship that the coach has to utilise when he is devising training schemes for individuals. Here are a few more points to consider:

1. *Postural movement.* How does posture – straight, crouched, twisted – affect the pace and power of the individual? What are the restrictions placed on the range of movement by posture? How does the range of head movement affect the range of body movement?
2. *Shaped movement.* Does the opponent move in short, sharp, angular movements or long, smooth and curved? Can the individual do both or only one? Which one? Is the movement pattern different when doing standing and ground grappling, or is it the same?

The novice has got to be helped to produce his own – known and understood – movement vocabulary

An element which cannot be ignored even at this low level of learning is the aesthetic. Does effective movement need to be aesthetically pleasing? Can an efficient throwing action be ugly? The short answer to the last question, anyway, in the short term, is of course yes. In that case the next question will need to be, can an ugly, effective action be repeated and repeated and stay effective and ugly? I have a suspicion that it cannot. Now of course the meaning of 'ugly' and 'aesthetically pleasing' has to be discussed.

Environmental shapes, cultural schemata and group expectations (to say nothing of innate propensities) have much to do with what an individual considers as being aesthetically right. His understanding and interpretation of these various symbols and images will be heavily influenced by his early nurturing and so shape him aesthetically for the rest of his life.§ It can be easily imagined that the verticality of the Germanic forests helped to produce the Gothic style of architecture, the image of paradise greatly influenced

Islamic art; and possibly the best illustrations of symbolism are the core symbols of Christianity and Buddhism as represented by the deaths of their respective founders. Christianity is very vertical and aggressive,* while Buddhism is horizontal and passive. In time of course they come to mean more than just those simple qualities, but they have influenced greatly the thinking of anyone brought up in those respective cultures. One is aggressive co-operation, the other tolerant opposition. As the artist, the interpreter of reality as art, must not be misled by his cultural prejudices, so the coach, the interpreter of reality as skill, must not be misled by his traditional prejudices. For example, it is often heard in judo technical circles that 'smooth' supple actions are better than 'jerky' stiff ones. Nonsense, of course. In the same way that beauty is not restricted to smoothness, so neither is effectiveness restricted to smoothness.** Effectiveness is a matter of harmony, harmony is to do with beauty, beauty is to do with a practical appreciation of an effect and human effect is to do with proficiency through repetition and feedback; repetition produces a skill and a skill is effectiveness.

Having got the novice to appreciate some of the value and qualities of different movement patterns and rhythms, the coach can show how competitive skills flow 'naturally' from these patterns. For example, the most common time to inject an attacking action into a movement pattern is on a change of direction. Not only is there a dramatic drop in pace (sometimes even a stop), but when the control is great (when the discrepancy between skills is great) then the 'unstable' throws can be used (i.e. *uchimata, haraigoshi* etc.). When the difference in skills is very slight, then the blocking or rotating throws are best used (i.e. *taiotoshi, seoi-nage* etc.). There is a dance-like quality about this type of training and in the early stages there will need be an organised degree of co-operation between the two novices. Each one must learn how to establish the movement-pattern opportunities for the advantage of the other.

---

　* The first Christian symbol, the fish, was horizontal. Perhaps it was not aggressive enough for the later militant Christians, who saw their task as being to take their religion to the rest of the world.
　** Is the angularity of the Chinese style (i.e. Sesshu) any less effective than the Japanese style (i.e. Tani Buncho) when assessing Japanese brushwork?§

A by the way

Jigoro Kano, the founder of judo, saw judo mainly as a social training for the citizen. Like many other foreign liberal educationalists, especially physical educationalists at the turn of the century, he was a patriot and believed that a nation's people should be prepared to defend their rights and privileges against any foreign oppression.§ To do that the citizen would need to be fit and his programme of physical education (which included judo) would help him do that. It was in this context that he taught judo as self-defence; not as a parochial training for a back-alley squabble,* but as a microcosmic reflection of the spirit needed for national defence. Much the same attitude can be found in the English physical education Acts from 1904 to 1933.§

Also, like those same other national educationalists, Kano did not trust competition. He, like them, felt that too much stress placed on competition would produce people who were selfish, greedy, narcissistic and full of hubris; in short, as Herbert Spencer said, competition can re-barbarise the participant. So Kano tried to play down the importance of competition and stressed the necessity of structured learning (*kata*), but unfortunately his efforts were not very successful – contest skills did become the major objective. *Randori*, spontaneous competition (thanks largely to the attitude of the Japanese army in the 1930s), became the backbone of judo training, with structured, co-operative training as supplementary.§

During the journey from Japan to Britain this element of co-operation seems to have faded even more and perhaps never made landfall. There is little co-operation or help-giving in British judo circles now. There may well be many instances of individuals offering advice on how to 'correct' someone else's technique, but no-one is asked, or expected to give up training time to help others. If real progress is to be made at all stages of learning and training, situations

---

* Most judo leaders have completely misunderstood the concept of self-defence in judo. It has always been seen in the very narrow and crude form – fighting without weapons in some kind of street brawl. Reading Kano's ideology it is quite evident that he was not referring to it in this narrow sense, but in the wider contest of sustaining the Yamato spirit of Japan. This was confirmed to me by Mr Takasaki (his son-in-law), who held the same patriotric attachment. Not the patriotism of fascist or imperialistic nationalism but the patriotism of a man who feels his country has evolved something – a culture – that can benefit the rest of the world.

will need be set up where specific circumstances will give the trainees a particular skill experience, which perhaps will help to improve their ability. As the skill standard improves, so will the complexity of the structured situations need to be made more comprehensive. There will be no question of trainees being capable of producing such structured situations 'off the top of their heads'. They will need careful rehearsal. That will demand a degree of unselfishness not asked of judo people at present. They will be asked to learn skills (at a low level, it is true) that will only marginally help their own skills, but in the main will be for the benefit of others; yet of course, if the others improve, it means they will all improve – 'ji ta kyo ei' – and that's what Kano wanted judo to be all about. At the moment, there is too much competition. It is all competition! Certainly in my mind there is no doubt that such an imbalance contributes to some degree to the amount of acrimony within the sport of judo. Judo could certainly do with a lot more co-operation and harmony and a lot less competition and conflict.

Some simple tactics

It can be very exciting to make the teaching of tactics take up the first few lessons of a beginner's introductory course to judo. I have already queried the justification for making technique the first item on the beginner's menu and suggested that an alternative could be skill. Now I go further and suggest that on occasion skill can also be replaced by something else as an *hors d'oeuvres* – tactics. Again it would depend upon the physical aptitude of the group, but providing they could move intelligently and imaginatively there is no reason why they could not learn skills through tactics.

What are tactics? In very simple terms, a sequence of moves imposed on an opponent to bring about a particular set of circumstances that will facilitate a winning attack.§ In the first instance the pair will need to *act* the movement pattern; for example the attacker first pulls the opponent forward (by himself going backwards); the pace is quite slow because it would be difficult to pull the opposition forward fast. Suddenly the attacker changes and instead of pulling, pushes the opponent quickly backwards. After a few steps the opponent reacts by slowing up his retreating movement and then by pushing forward.

It is put to the novices, how would they make an opponent move backwards after moving forward? They should get the idea (but if not, tell them) that an attack is the obvious answer. What sort of an attack? An attack that tries to throw the opponent backwards. Some kind of *ouchi* could be shown (whether a name is given or not is quite immaterial). So he retreats and then he begins to resist by pushing forward. Now is the time for the winning-attack throw – let's say *taiotoshi*. The sequence is simple, realistic – in terms of conditions – and it shows the novice clearly what can be achieved by tactics. The coach could make up many of these simple structured situations (the above *ouchi/taiotoshi* is a typical novice's *kata*), incorporating various elements necessary for an evolving learning group. The people within the group will have discovered much about what goes to make up a total judo skill;* the change of pace and of direction, the opportunities that creates, how scoring affects throwing actions, the difference between skills and techniques. It should have been an imaginative and edifying process.

Having said all that, having made the point – strongly I hope – that there should be several kinds of beginners' introductory courses, each course built to suit a particular type of person, it must be realised this may be quite impossible to do in practice. There can be many reasons: lack of time, perhaps the club or centre has not the time to programme several beginners' courses (however worthwhile they are); lack of facilities, there may not be enough mat-space for several courses *and* the normal training opportunities; there may not be enough support from the management group, they may say that all that novice time would unbalance the club's total training programme; the coach himself may not have the knowledge or the wherewithal to run such a multi-choice group of novices' courses. So be it, the coach is back to square one and he can only run one beginners' introductory course. Life seldom offers all and the practical man has got to make the best of what is given him. With luck, therefore, if it is a matter of only one course, the coach will try to incorporate all or most of what has been outlined above. There must be imaginative problems for the curious to solve, there must be spoon-feeding for those who want support, tactics for those with 'cross-word puzzle' minds, technique for those who want discipline, and for those who want skills, explanations about what is happening. Structured situations (*kata*), co-operation throughout the group, individual help – meaning here not just the coach helping everyone

---

* A total judo skill is that which refers to the conduct of a competitor, which needs to last the whole of a judo match – a skill that lasts for 3 to 15 minutes.

but the novices helping each other (sometimes one novice can 'teach' the group some sequence he has prepared*) – are all needed. What it is important to recognise is that beginners' courses should not be rigid, as some coaches try to make them, but flexible learning units, each one shaped to the needs of the people that fill those units. If a programme content has to be made up for purposes of advertisements (e.g. in local newspapers) or for approval (e.g. by an education authority), then general headings can be used, i.e. introduction to tactics etc., which will allow the necessary flexibility. It may even be of value if the length of the course is variable, giving say a minimum and a maximum duration. Again, other factors may prohibit such an approach; an obvious one is economics, but it is the non-rigidity of approach that is important. To reiterate what was said at the beginning, what the novice learns in the first few weeks of his judo life will stay with him for ever. It is worth the coach spending a lot of time deciding what he is going to put into those first few weeks.

What is a good coach?

A top judo competitor was once asked why he had lost an important match? He replied, 'It's my coach, he reminds me of my father and I hate the pair of them.' Seriously, a coach's function changes as the performer's standard improves, yet paradoxically enough his role stays the same. The coach, in the main, is an avuncular supportive figure; he offers advice (on most things), with luck hopefully provides short cuts to success and a vicarious experience that the competitor has not yet had time to collect; finally he is a fund of technical expertise.§ The emphasis on which of these qualities the coach provides should vary as the performer matures. Early on in the business of acquiring skills, the trainee will usually want technical expertise and occasionally counselling. Later when he has competitive success he may want more counselling than technical expertise. While that is what the performer wants, it may not be what the coach wants to give. A controversial issue at the present time, both among coaches and those who debate the coaches' role, is – should coaches have responsibilities to the performer outside the training hall?§

---

* As St Augustine said, the best way to learn is to teach. If a trainee were given a very simple teaching task (i.e. a change of direction attack) and say a week's preparation time and then allowed to take the group through the sequence he had worked out, it would certainly teach him a lot about sequence skills.

Those who say no suggest that not only does the coach not have the training for such a function, but ethically he has no need to guide on anything other than technical matters. Others, and I am on this side, suggest that as a coach he has already accepted the task – and the responsibility – of altering an individual's personality; he cannot abnegate it when it does not suit him, or when the responsibility becomes uncomfortable. Generally the trainee is both willing and prepared to pass many of his decision – making processes over to the coach, so that he can dedicate himself totally to the task of improving his skills. Having accepted that obligation the coach cannot simply ignore it when circumstances become difficult or unpopular.

The coach's own ideology and philosophy will sooner or later impinge on the trainee in various ways – if only through how the skills are taught and by the examples set by the coach in terms of behaviour and expectations. The coach is older and (should be) wiser than the trainee who usually needs an avuncular figure that he can rely on, and because of this relationship the trainee is much influenced by the coach. It is therefore desirable that the coach has qualities that will benefit both the individual and society in the long run. That is, he should be honest and sincere, have a hunger for knowledge and be aware that teaching others is a great 'ego-trip' and admit that he enjoys every moment of that god-like position. To refute this truism can lead to much false modesty and can be both sickening and unctuous. Finally, he must be able to keep sport in its true perspective – a means to a living and not a dead end.

Sport can now be, and is, used as an expansion of the spirit of insurrection and anarchy. What began as a coach's exhortation to his team – 'winning is not everything, it is the only thing' – and caused a wry smile among the idealists, has become the slogan of the sport-vandal. What was the accusation of the cynic, that sport is the exercise of the philistine, has become the assumption of the public. I am sure the democratic Athenian did not contemplate the insidiousness of his slave-state and the fact that it could bring his civilisation down (which it did) any more than the Western man contemplates that sport could bring *his* civilisation down.§ Yet sport could well act as a substitute for that slave-stratum and by its function as a purveyor of insidious ideologies and expectations bring down western civilisation. One of the few people who could buttress against this line of development and guide sport back to its earlier and more congenial purpose in society is the coach. The proviso is that he will need to have a sense of social responsibility, of social justice, and a broad awareness of his role in evolving sport, which because of the already changed status of sport in society will include a political element. So the coach will need to be technical adviser, accepter of social responsibilities and political guide. He can achieve all that by his own efforts, but it would be better if there were a national coaching institution where he could be trained methodically.

Chapter 4
The Psychology of Competition, or How to Make the Most out of Very Little

'The coach, with 20 years judo teaching experience, was told that kata *was good for contest experience, and it should be taught. As he knew nothing about* kata, *the claim could be true, and it was very Japanese, which made the suggestion even more plausible. Who knows, he thought, he might well be able to "con" his followers with it and it could also be used to patch over some of his own areas of ignorance. Psychologically too it would add another plank to the structure of Japanese mysticism in Judo. He decided. Good, he would teach it.'*

The psychology of sport has a fascination for both the theoretical investigator and the pragmatist coach. The coach feels it can provide an insight into that aspect of skilled performance that practical experience will never give him; while the theorists – like physical educationalists – feel it will explain physical skills in a way that surpasses practical experience. These expectations are quite acceptable and indeed are a part of any legitimate study of physical skills, provided of course it is realised that no ultimate statements will be made about what constitutes physical skills.

Research students, investigating some obscure aspect of a sports skill, will be overheard to say that they hope their final thesis will not gather dust on some forgotten shelf, but will make a realistic contribution to the coaching profession. A worthy and respected hope, but one which in many ways is arrogant, for who ever uncovers the original source? It is the learning that has taken place that will greatly outweigh the importance of some ephemeral conclusion about a bit of limited research. It is the discipline of the research that benefits the individual and eventually other people as well. Similarly with the coach, if he should stumble across some apparently new pearl of wisdom, he should not get too superior because it will almost certainly have been found at least once before. Certainly he cannot assume he has found a resting place in his search for knowledge, as so many coaches do once they have become 'coaches'. Like the researcher, it is the knowledge that has been acquired in the search for the pearl of wisdom rather than the pearl itself that is important. Galileo was chastised by Mother Church, not because he taught that the earth went round the sun (a matter of interpretation anyway), but because by disagreeing with the Church he confirmed that knowledge was infinite, and therefore the Church had no monopoly over it.§ The form is finite, not the content.

The psychology of intent

One of the first questions that need be asked when advocating the pursuit of knowledge is, is it wanted? How much do sports people want to know about their sport, when they are progressing through it? Just enough technical knowledge to ensure that progress takes place, or enough all-round technical knowledge to do that and to satisfy a general curiosity regarding the integration of sport with society? Many educationalists will insist that education – in its democratic sense – is what sport should be promulgating. All trainees, they say, should be taught or trained to think and act for themselves, to take part in the educational process, led by the leaders – the coaches.§ It is of course a lovely idealistic intent, but coaches know that many performers want nothing to do with 'education', they just want to do the skills and preferably win and/or earn money.* There is nothing wrong with that; why should not other people help them do what they want to do? Just as some people try to suggest there should be no politics in sport, others want no education in sport. If it is wrong to impose a religious ideology upon people who are not interested in religion, is it not wrong to impose education on those sportspeople who wish to remain ignorant?

---

§ When this mark is found, it means that there is a 'further reading' section in the bibliography.

* Sport in its new role of international entertainment is not only providing a source of much wealth for some but a problem for others in readjusting their priorities. Show business has encapsulated its ethical priorities in the aphorism 'the show must go on'; sport has not yet found its equivalent.

Jigoro Kano, the founder of judo, was very much the educationalist. There is no doubt that he saw judo as an education (witness his two famous maxims – see glossary). Judo in the narrrow sense, what Kano called competitive judo, would, he believed, brutalise the participants if there were no compensatory measures. It was an opinion shared by Herbert Spencer, who said the same thing about sport in general; it would 're-barbarise' the participants. Kano knew Spencer as he knew Mill, by study, therefore Kano advocated judo in the wide sense, judo as a form of self-help, of mutual benefit, as a more community-orientated Utilitarianism. It was a development that found echoes in other countries – Dewey in America, Sedgwick in England, Lestgaft in Russia, all evolving from the determinism of John Stuart Mill.§

It is a view which I myself share strongly. Judo (sport too) is a way to broaden the individual's horizons and to nurture responsibilities to society. Once the skills of judo or sport become an end in themselves, then degeneracy has begun. But perhaps that is because I was taught judo in such a manner. My judo coach, or more appropriately I should say teacher, imposed upon me a curiosity for learning that I have never been able to shake off since those long-gone days. Judo training for him—and therefore for me—certainly did not stop at the *dojo* walls. He would take me off to the theatre, opera, concerts and exhibitions. I was then expected to write analytical essays on all the events. These essays were discussed. Book lists were presented to me and I had to work my way through them. Again debate was held on every one of them. Judo training for me was as much a university education as a physical discipline and the skills acquired through the latter earnt me a scholarship to the Kodokan Judo Institute in Tokyo. Once there the education continued, because not only was I made a research student of the Kodokan but I lived with Kano's son-in-law and family where I learnt much about Kano's philosophy. So it is easy to see why I feel judo should be educational, but I accept that some others will not want to see it like this and will prefer it as an end in itself. As long as the skill works for them from time to time in competition, that is good enough – no more is expected from the training.* For me, however, that would be too limiting, too boring and make training a

---

* For some the semi-mystical experience of throwing without being aware of throwing is promoted to the apogee of skilled performance and therefore the only thing of value in judo training is just that; all else is ignored. An extreme example of Kano's 'judo in the narrow sense'.

stodgy mixture of muscle and blood that I would find difficult to take. Everyone to his or her tastes of course.

The coach is the one who determines whether training is educational or vocational. Like the performer (and frequently he is something of an ex-performer) he will also have a preference or a propensity for expanding or contracting his knowledge – with or without the aid of judo.§ If the curious performer finds himself in a group controlled by a non-curious coach, he may well have many problems. In the opening stages, of course, such a trainee will have difficulty learning the skills as the coach teaches them, for attitudes will be so polarised. Later, naturally, the schism will become wider, because the range of subjects will be that much greater; for example, the many forms of moral issues will proliferate, i.e. should there be gamesmanship, rule-breaking, intentional injury to the opponent. Therefore the individual may find that he will have to leave that group and coach and find himself a more congenial set-up. It is well known in judo circles how certain coaches have about them a group that reflects their own characteristics and attitudes. If the coach's range of technique is limited, then the group's techniques will be limited; if the coach is intellectually alive, so will be the group. It is for this kind of reason that those who are responsible for organising parts of sport like, for example, national squads, should keep this development well in mind. If they wish to have a future generation of coaches who are dull and unimaginative then all that is needed is to appoint dull and unimaginative coaches to train the contemporary generation of performers. If the controlling body wants to make the most of what it has, it will need to put training – in all its forms – in the hands of imaginative, curious and cultured coaches.

Why do people want to perform in top sport? It is an intriguing phenomenon; my own research raised several points that caused me much cogitation. At first glance the motivation to do sport (whatever that means) appears simple enough; to win or succeed.§ Yet is it? Very few in my sample of sports champions gave this as their reason, either for starting or continuing. Is it for what the humanistic psychologists call intrinsic motivation, the satisfaction obtained from the knowledge that one's skills are improving (not necessarily that they are better than someone else's)? Again few admitted to being interested in getting their skills better, so why then do they do it?

The question is to do with 'motivation'; how the coach responds to the needs of that individual's motivation will decide the form the teaching will take. As we are dealing with people there will of course be all kinds of motivation; certainly some men will be driven by the need to win – to overcome opposition; others will do it for the satisfaction of ever-improving performances, but will these be the majority?§ I would suggest maybe not. It would appear that many sportsmen are very existentialist. They live for the day: few concern themselves about what they will do when they are finished with sport/judo; few will concern themselves with long-term planning of any kind (that's why they want a coach, for he can do that for them). Sartre, that arch-existentialist, seems to have an understanding of sportsmen that few other philosophers have. He suggests that sportsmen have intentions rather than motivations§ (he queries the whole concept of motivation) and that these intentions can be deterministic (having a purpose or goal) or non-deterministic (having no goal or purpose) and perhaps the latter is more common than the former. He suggests the intention of skill acquisition is to *be*, to be in the sense of being accepted as a special kind of person, to be an individual different from other individuals with an individuality that is singular. Certainly many of the champions I have interviewed have expressed as their main aspiration that they want to be recognised, want to be known by their name, want to be known as skilful performers – not because the performance is necessarily important but because the skill makes them identifiable as someone special. Can the urge to be recognised be called non-deterministic? Does not being recognised qualify as intent? Possibly not, for in the early stages of training it is not expressed as a need, certainly not articulated and probably not a part of the group's expectations and therefore does not rate as 'orientated thought'. At the early stage of skill training, the need has not matured enough to be felt as directional, it is simply applied concern. But more specifically, such a trainee merely feels the need to dedicate, he is not interested in what the dedication will produce for him (in terms of 'profit'), only that it will prove to him that he *is*, he exists. It is that 'dedication' which gradually and eventually evolves into the more recognisable form, that of being recognised.

Such an obtuse intention, void of 'normal' purpose, need not impinge on the everyday awareness of the individual's self-existence. At that level the individual may well consider – and rightly so – that he has no motivation or even intention. That conclusion could be disturbing, for the individual, being part of the Western logico-rational tradition, may consider that to do something without knowing why it is done is tantamount to being slightly crazy. Therefore, to correct this self-assessment, he may quickly seize on the motivation suggested to him by his peer group or the coach, i.e. to win, to get gold medals, self-gratification etc. However, because these are rather second-hand values, the player may not attach a great deal of significance to them (they could simply act as a convenient justification for doing what he was doing should he suddenly be called upon to justify his action); therefore when he is under undue stress, before a major event for example, he may abandon all pretence that winning is his motivation and adopt a totally indifferent attitude to the coming event. The coach, to say nothing of the peer group, who has assumed that the 'normal' stimulant to win is still the force within the competition, suddenly finds all that orthodoxy has evaporated. The coach is stunned! He is faced with an inexplicable situation; what is he to do? Shout, scream, throw the man out of the team? To get the most out of what he has got, the coach has got to make major efforts to discover what it is that drives his squad members. He cannot assume any longer that the issue is simply that the men just want to win (although they may). There might be many other motive forces. If the coach wants a man to win he may well need to treat him in a way that the performer does not expect – for example, that the coach does not want him to win. The coach may have to change his approach entirely, if he wants to get the most from his trainee.

In this business of 'motivation' there is another culture-clash that can also cause confusion.§ It has been mentioned how the Western tradition of logic influences those nurtured in it. Such logic is concerned with sequentialism. Such a tradition does not exist in the mysterious Orient; indeed, such intellectual systems as Zen do everything possible to confuse the whole concept of sequence (usually with great success). Koan Zen is like Socratic interrogation turned inside out. Socrates would ask questions that could be answered only after logical/sequential thought; the Koan came in a

nonsensical question form, e.g. what is the sound of one hand clapping, which could not be answered in the normal run of reality, but it made two simple points: a question does not necessarily presuppose an answer; and if conventional reality/logic is changed, then perhaps an answer is conceivable.

The yin-yang logogram symbolises the paradox of the opposites.
One is quite distinct from the other, yet both are interlocked and there is some of one in the midst of the other.

The yin-yang logogram is both representative and symbolic of the interaction that goes on between two opposites (any opposite). Each difference has its respective advantage and disadvantage as related to the other. So in the ways of developing attitudes; the Socratic method is good for future planning and anticipation, bad for dealing with the unusual and the unexpected, whereas the Koan approach is good for responding to the unexpected in an organised manner, but poor when it comes to dealing with long-lasting problems. Good sport performers know how they can train for the long-lasting problem and know they can often deal with the unexpected, but they do not know how to train for that – the ability is somewhat frightening because they do not understand it. It is mysterious and that points to the esoteric and that in turn means, for many, the Orient. If the sport is very Western, like tennis or golf, then an oriental factor may have to be forcibly injected into the skill preparation to explain it all, hence the inauguration of 'inner sport'.* If the sport already has an Eastern ingredient (like judo, karate etc.) then that can be exploited for all it's worth. However, the clash of the two approaches – Western pragmatism and Eastern illogicality — can cause confusion, particularly when the approaches that produce that clash are not even realised, let alone understood.§

In judo perhaps the best example of the sound of two cultures clashing is *uchikomi*. The contribution from the West is thinking and from the Orient a unique approach to the appraisal of skill. The idea of 'thought' in a Western context is entangled with the body-mind concept which has swung its way through the writings of people like St Augustine, Aquinas, Locke, Mill. The early bifurcation had something to do with Utopia (heaven) and life after death; Aquinas, for example, suggested there is a different mode of understanding after the death of the body, but later in the nineteenth century John Stuart Mill had changed the context and was talking of the body as the medium for sensations.§ Be that as it may, this long tradition of duality has had the effect of separating thinking from the body and this dichotomy in turn has produced various misleading images. To give but one example, there is the 'brain as telephone exchange' image, which still moulds many people's thoughts on ___

---

* Inner sport is an eclectic coaching system utilising ideas of Zen, yoga, transcendental meditation, humanistic psychology and inspired guesswork (which therefore can go wrong). It has attractive characteristics but needs to mature.

thinking. The model is as follows: a sensation is experienced on the outskirts of the body system, whereupon messages are flashed up to the exchange-panel, the brain. There the messages are intercepted, translated and decisions taken, based on that translation. Those decisions are then flashed back along the nerve-lines to where sensation was originally felt and then action is implemented. Just as the medieval philosopher used the idea that thought was independent of body in order to support his contention about heaven, so some modern coaches utilise the out-of-date telephone exchange image to support their contention that skill contains no thought. In practice, this means they use the following argument – an opportunity for an attack is seen; the Pony Express rider complete with message charges along well-worn trails to the brain; there the messages are read and decisions made and put into action, communiqués are given back to the Pony Express man and he gallops off to initiate the attack. The coaches who draw this exciting image make the point that the process takes too long and before the message gets back to initiate the action, the opportunity has long gone; therefore – they claim – skill must be beyond the range of thinking, and functions in a non-thinking manner. They go on to say that you must somehow feel, instinctively become aware of the opportunity, and so it is possible to attack instantly. A reasonable conclusion, of course, if the 'Pony Express' picture is correct (although I wonder how 'feelings' and 'instincts' function without some form of thinking?), but what happens if that imagery is totally spurious?

Gilbert Ryle made a resounding counter-attack on dualism and maintained that monism was the more likely model of action. He proposed that thinking is movement or, rephrased with a slightly different emphasis, that mental (silent) verbalisation and movement are two different functions of the one process (thinking). The action of movement is not the result of thinking but is an intrinsic part of the thinking process.§ Ryle showed, as other radical thinkers have shown in other spheres of knowledge, that mechanistic explanations of human function are extremely hazardous and almost always spurious. Knowledgeable speculations have now abandoned images like telephone exchanges to exemplify the brain and have begun to see 'thinking' as the highly complex business it obviously is. Some authorities have suggested that perhaps there are subsidiary thinking centres scattered throughout the body that, although they are an integral part of the central thinking system (the brain), can in some degree function independently. Another startling development has emerged from the work done on brain bisection. For various medical reasons, not relevant here, experiments have been made where the cutting of the links between the two halves of the brain has been the central act. Intriguing queries have been formulated. Take the most bizarre: it would seem that each dissociated half (of the brain) can operate the body almost entirely independently of the other half. If so, does that mean the body is being operated by two separate minds, independent of each other, but at the same time? An impressive manifestation of the yin-yang principle in neurology! To take this line of puzzlement one stage further, it is accepted that even in a 'normal' person the links between the two brain halves are more effective co-operation than essential coexistence, so in essence would the same query apply to 'normal' people? Is one body being run by two minds? If so, would that explain schizophrenia? As Nagel writes: 'The natural conception of a single person controlled by a mind possessing a single visual field, individual facilities for each of the other senses, unitary systems of memory, desire, belief and so forth, may come into conflict with the physiological facts when it is applied to ourselves.'

Such a drastic change in conception plays havoc with the notion of telephone exchanges and whether 'seeing' opportunities automatically insinuates inappropriateness of attacking action. Opportunity in the context of brain bisection could mean an analogy with an intellectual range-finder; each half would instantly register the circumstance and the instant correlation of the two registrations – confirming that the opportunity did in fact exist – would fire off the action (movement). It has to be admitted the model is different, right or wrong, and shows that no model of 'thinking' can be treated as sacrosanct. As knowledge is acquired, 'factual conglomerates' fall apart and then are reassembled in an entirely new way.

Another fascinating hypothesis that indirectly impinges on this business of thinking and action is that the invention of the printing press did not only help in the promulgation of information but nurtured the present widely-held belief that thinking must be sequential. The presentation of the printed page, by its very two-dimensional quality, indoctrinated people to think sequentially – even if they had not done so before. Reading, particularly silent mental reading, made people assume that mental verbalisation *is* thinking; it is not. Musicians do not think in words and then translate them into sound any more than an artist thinks in words and translates them into colour. Wittgenstein brought home to philosophy how insidious words can be; words can be mistaken for objects,

objects misconceived through words: 'A name means an object: the object is its meaning' (*Tractatus*).

Pre-reading thinking may well have been of a completely different type to post-reading thinking. Maybe it is why illiterate or semi-literate sportsmen have a different approach to skill performance than educated ones – and why educated coaches have difficulty appreciating what the illiterate are trying to do. Perhaps it is why blind people have different ways of tackling learning. Perhaps it is the obvious reason why a champion can never articulate about his skill, simply because he never has verbalised it before – he thinks/does it; he has never silently 'read' it.

If there is any veracity in there being such complex forms of skill-performance, it would necessitate a complete reassessment of what is an attacking opportunity. The whole process of see-transmit-translate-transmit-action would be made redundant and in its place a simple think-act syndrome substituted. It would make much more sense to the top performer. His empiricism would tell him – oh so clearly – that his skill must be modifiable instantly to suit ever-changing conditions. He cannot therefore depend on some subconscious system which is beyond his conscious control. He must be in a position whereby he can consciously influence his decision-making process at any instant throughout an attack. The thinking process is keyed into action not verbalisation. He is aware of what is happening everywhere. There may be occasions when for conscious reasons some control is lost. For example, in biomechanical terms a ballistic movement may be consciously initiated and it goes beyond control by its mechanical nature; similarly a thought pattern may be initiated laterally to the main thought-stream and its momentum will temporarily interrupt the main stream, so causing a fleeting loss of control.* But the competitor must learn to ignore the lapses and

---

* In this context I prefer using De Bono's nomenclature, i.e. 'lateral thinking', to early Freudian, i.e. 'subconscious', because it creates a better image of what is happening. Lateral thinking is taking place consciously but simultaneously and parallel to the main stream of consciousness. A classic example of this lateral-skill-performance is the 'throw-done-without-thinking', a phenomenon often quoted, in judo circles as the example *par excellence* of what the epitome of judo training is all about and why there is no need to think while training. It is not that there is no thinking, only that it functions parallel to the main stream of thinking/action.

train on the knowledge that he is in control at all times. He must be able to produce skills to order, at a particular time and place, therefore he must be able to *think* his way through them. In training, therefore, the performer must be taught to recognise opportunities and what sort of skill to use for them.

Now the contribution, to *uchikomi*, from the East. Skill for the Japanese (in whatever form it takes) is the effective resolution of a situation that appears to be spontaneous but must be easily recognised as being the result of much training. Skill for them is not so much a process that achieves success in terms of one person dominating another, as the personification of a particular ideology. If skill is used as domination (i.e. to beat other people) it becomes a force. Japanese idealism, encapsulated in the *samurai* image, mistrusts such force. Mishima quotes the *Hagakure*: 'A man who earns a reputation for being skilled at a technical art is idiotic. Because of his foolishness in concentrating his energies on one thing, he has become good at it by refusing to think of anything else. Such a person is of no use at all.'

The ideal samurai did not see skill as a challenge, something which he had to master and be better at than everybody else. The samurai's task as a soldier was very simple: it was not to achieve a high level of skill with a sword or spear, it was to die – when and where his feudal lord told him. Skill for the samurai was concerned with the style of dying.§

Zen Buddhism has been the fountainhead of Japanese ideology, particularly for the samurai, since its importation into Japan in the twelfth century. It has pontificated on all matters vegetable, animal and mineral – cultural – since that time. It was to be expected therefore that Zen would make an authoritative statement on skill and it tackled the task in the same way it defined its own metaphysical attitudes, from the conviction that total commitment was the only way to achieve mastery of the self – through the skill, not of the skill. For Zen was concerned, not with samurai sport (for the Japanese have no conception of sport*) but with samurai death. The samurai's *raison d'être* was not to win competitions but to die. Zen's job was to make that act as effective a part of the samurai's service to his lord as possible. To quote Mishima again, 'Anyone who is

---

* In the book by Nakamura the author makes the point very strongly that sport is not a concept found in the national language; if the idea has to be purveyed the English word 'sport' has to be used.§

especially skilled in a particular art is a technician, not a samurai.' The samurai's attitude to skill and to life in general is summed up dramatically in the adage found in the *Hagakure*, 'I discovered that the Way of the Samurai is Death.'

This interpretation of skill, as a medium for death, is bound to contain some degree of ritual. Just as the original purpose of any army drill was to bring the soldier to the point of death with the least amount of time to think about it, so with the ritual in the samurai's training method. Ritual would get him to the point of extinction with the least thinking time.

So here are two disparate cultural attitudes all set for a head-on collision. *Uchikomi* is a repetitive physical exercise, in which only a part of a throwing technique is practised and done in the form of a ritual: a learning by rote. As far as the Eastern intention is concerned the exercise is to eliminate conscious verbalisation and produce a habitual movement throughout only half the range of the technique. This is in line with traditional samurai thinking which maintains that terminal effectiveness is dependent upon spontaneous thinking produced by mind-dulling ritual. The Western contribution is to say that a living skill must be capable of being reproduced exactly the same – but differently – for as many times as needed (that is a bit of occidental mysticism for a change). Which approach has the most veracity when related to the sportsman's ideal objective and which one will obscure the other when related to the sportsman's competitive objective? The performer will need to decide.§

How is the best to be made out of *uchikomi* if it is to help in the business of skill acquisition? The following modifications are suggested:

1. The 'thrower' should vary the parts of the technique he rehearses by repetition i.e. the movement *before* the attacking movement starts and the movement *after* the attacking movement finishes.
2. The partner should not stay still in the one position; as the 'thrower' repeats a particular part of a technique the partner should move every time into a slightly different position,* so the 'thrower' can experience the need to change his movement slightly to fit the changed condition.

Many instructors in the past have felt the inadequacies of

---

* Another example of the mutual obligation of trainee to trainee is to help each other by positive conscientious co-operation.

traditional *uchikomi* and have tried to improve matters by altering certain aspects of the exercise – but seldom knowing why they are changing what they are changing. The most drastic alteration became known as '*uchikomi*-on-the-move'; the change is obvious enough, but simply moved the error from standing still to moving. Because there was a lack of understanding the faults of static repetition were simply extended into the moving form, the main one being that the partner offers the same opportunity every time, thus encouraging the 'thrower' to do the same attacking movement every time. For skills to improve, opportunity and attack must vary frequently.

If *uchikomi* is the sound of two cultures clashing, what is the sound of one culture clash? *Kata*! *Kata* seems to have but one cultural origin but instead has the spirit of many within it. *Kata* means form and in the daily parlance of the Japanese can mean shape, referring to the shape of any mundane object, but it also has a profounder meaning – form as being.§ Kano considered *kata* an extremely important part of judo training but certainly had no monopoly of the idea; nor did the Japanese as a whole, and it is here where the taste of other cultures can be found. Presumably the most well-known speculator on form was Plato. He found the idea of life being in a permanent state of flux an abhorrent one.§ In order to reassure himself that there was some kind of permanency somewhere, he devised the doctrine of form. Plato proposed that form was the essence of reality, it was unchanging and perfect and beyond space and time. However, he still had to accommodate the actuality that change played a large part in existence, so he further suggested that content – that which made up form – was changeable. Karl Popper was very suspicious of many of the implications contained in Plato's theory of ideas or form and accused it of being the seed-bed for many later social evils, for example totalitarianism and historicism.§ If these suspicions could be transferred to the judo *kata* scene, they would be substantiated. Over the last twenty years or so *kata* has been treated as absolute, fixed both in form and content for ever; the approach has spawned a fine set of dogmas – all opposed to the business of skill improvement.

A little to the east of Plato's Greece could be found that fascinating religion of Light with its supreme One – Mazda and his prophet Zoroaster. Form was a central part of Zoroaster's teaching. Form – of which there were many varieties – came direct from Mazda and provided moulds for man's thought and behaviour. They were unchanging but Mazda filled them with 'rays of infinite light' to help man to realise the great range of content that was form.§ The commonality with Plato is noticeable: the form is constant, the content variable.

As is to be expected, China cannot be left out of such a subject. Indeed it made a very significant contribution to the doctrine of form and content. Several writers made scholarly commentaries on the doctrine, but undoubtedly the most important one, as far as judo is concerned anyway, was the neo-Confucian Shao Yung (1011 - 1077 A.D.) Shao saw the organisation of life in the form of a management pyramid: at the top was Tao, the Great One (unity transcends duality).*§ The Great One spawns two primary manifestations – motion and rest. At the third strata in the pyramid can be found the offspring of motion and rest, motion breeding yin and yang (the principle of existential interaction) while rest produces *ju* and *go* (the principles of existential manipulation).§ These principles in turn interacted and the yin yang produced heaven while *ju* and *go* brought forth the earth. Under-pinning this general structure was the idea that the principles were constrained by form/*kata* with the content/*ki* being unlimited.

Kano was undoubtedly much influenced by the writings of Shao,** and it is of course his principles that are found in Kano's *ju* and *go-no-kata*.*** So if the most is to be made out of *kata* training it would seem to be the best idea to follow the classic (traditional) wisdom which teaches that form is finite and content infinite, rather than the modern traditionalists who insist that both form and content are finite. Kano and his master Shao seem to be particularly relevant to the aspiring contest-winner, who must be able to modify the contents, i.e. positions of body etc., within the form of throwing. To expect him to learn a sequence of movements which allows for no variation must be unreasonable.

Of course Kano did not get all of his inspiration from the East (China). He got much from the West too (Europe). Like other Restoration intellectuals Kano was much influenced by Victorian Utilitarianism, particularly that of John Stuart Mill and Herbert

---

* An oriental version of that occidental medieval aphorism known as Occam's Razor, plurality is not to be posited without necessity.

** Several Chinese neo-Confucians had a major influence on the Japanese intellectuals of the Restoration. In addition to Shao probably the other famous man of action was Wang Yang Ming. He believed in innate talent and that the mind is developed through the body. No wonder the Japanese liked him!§

*** Unfortunately the *go-no-kata* has been lost.

Spencer.* This influence had begun while Kano was at university in Tokyo, where both the principal and vice-principal were ardent Anglophiles. Kato, the principal, had translated much of the work of Mill and made it the core text of the humanities courses at the university. Kato also insisted that the *lingua franca* of the university should be English and many lectures were given in English. Kano, graduating in English and politics (1877 - 1882), would have been right in the middle of this whirlpool of English culture.§ On leaving university he was selected as being a potential member of the country's educational élite. As a part of his preparation for a top position within Japanese education he was appointed as lecturer and then vice-principal of the Gakushu In (the Peers School), the most prestigious training academy for the ruling class. He was then sent on a three-year study trip to Europe where he was expected to examine education in the main capitals.§ There he obtained first-hand experience of those doctrines he had studied in Japan. In France it was Rousseauism, in Berlin the Turnen group, the Ling movement in Sweden and in England Millsian influences on the London School Board. On his return to Japan he was promoted into the Civil Service where he gradually climbed up the ladder of power. In judo he tried to put Mill's theory of logic into physical form; the result was the *itsutsu-no-kata*. It stopped as a sequence of five movements, for the project was never completed; when the intention is appreciated this is not to be wondered at, particularly when the original inspiration is read.

For whatever reason, nurture or personal propensity, Kano had much sympathy with the Utilitarian doctrine; the two things he found most attractive were Mill's logic and his ideas on social obligation.** A paragraph from Mill's 'System of Logic' could very easily be an introduction to the *itsutsu-no-kata*: 'To ascertain therefore what are the laws of causation which exist in nature; to determine the effect of every cause and the cause of all effects is the main business of Induction; and to point out how this is done is the chief object of Inductive Logic.'§

Kano was trying to show that by studying specific principles in

---

* Spencer was not an 'official' Utilitarian, but was so much the personification of the Victorian ethos and supporter of Utilitarianism that to include him is no great distortion of fact.§

** This aspect of Mill's work was expanded significantly by later writers, Sidgwick, Moore and Rawls.

one context, the understanding engendered could be utilised for the better understanding of those same principles in other different forms. It is not an entirely spurious claim; by carefully studying the five principles he has managed to isolate in this *kata*, it can be seen how they can be utilised in skilful versions of certain techniques. Let me give a few examples:

The first principle. Dominant force (equivalent to *go*); here an unstoppable force is released to overpower the opponent. In competitive terms this is the simple frontal attack exemplified in such attacks as *uchimata, seoinage, haraigoshi* etc.

The second principle. Utilising force (equivalent to *ju*); here the out-of-control force used by an attacker is turned back on him to bring about his defeat. It is the perfect countering principle; such skills as *utsurigoshi* and *osotogaeshi* are classical examples of this principle.

The third principle. Centrifugal force; due to the nature of the way judo competitors grip each other and move, the circulating movements can very easily be converted into attacking force; skills utilising this effect are *hizaguruma, ashiguruma, tewaza* (of all types).

The fourth principle. Accelerating force; in competition it is frequently difficult to initiate a fast, powerful action from a static start, therefore it is necessary to build up force over a long period of time and movement; in competition the common way that is done is by a series of linked attacks (combination-attacks, *renraku waza*), e.g. a slow-paced *kouchi* is used, the opponent moves fairly quickly to avoid it, then a medium-paced *taiotoshi* is used, the opponent moves faster to avoid that and finally a fast ballistic *uchimata* is used for the terminal score.

The fifth principle. Existential force; a force that is a force by something being. This is the most profound of the five movements because it incorporates not only a particular type of force in physical skills but also force in that other greater growing concern of Kano – moral skills. In physical skills the principle is that by simply being in the way, by being, the moving force falls over it; in judo terms techniques like *sutemiwaza* are obvious examples and ones like *taiotoshi, seoinage, kouchi* are perhaps not so obvious examples. In moral terms, Kano is saying that if the individual is in the right place he may not have to do anything, his presence will be enough to create a moral force.*

It is an intriguing set of movements, and it is fascinating to speculate what other principles he would have isolated and how many he would have had in the full *kata*. What would he have called it, the *kata* of induction, the forms of being? It is interesting too to speculate what sort of *randori-no-kata* would have emerged if he had used the classification he devised in the *itsutsu-no-kata* to group grappling techniques. I am confident it would have added a whole new dimension to the analysis of competitive skills. So if you want to make the most out of the *itsutsu-no-kata*, study the form of classification and how it can affect the improvement of competitive skills.

Classification

Classification is an odd business. It has an affinity with that other, almost neurotic, propensity in man to compile 'natural laws' for all occasions. Karl Popper puts the point very well: 'Our intellect does not draw its laws from nature, but tries – with varying degrees of success – to impose upon nature laws which it freely invents.'§

So with classifications; we do not draw them from nature, but compile them for our convenience and then, with varying degrees of success, impose them on nature where none existed before. What happens then can be very stultifying, for that imposition seems to make them sacrosanct. What was originally just invention for convenience has become timeless and unchangeable. What is more, there is a rebound mechanism which is set in motion by that sempiternity and moulds future thinking. Already some of these rebounds have been noted, the moulding of thought patterns by the printed page, the establishment of aesthetic standards by ubiquitous advertising imagery. In judo there are many such examples; look at the way set titles in the *nage-no-kata* have affected analysis of technique. It has ossified throws like *taiotoshi* and *seoinage* for ever into one category (and totally ignored others like *kouchi*). To alter drastically the shape of these techniques is now tantamount to sacrilege. Kano's choice of the sub-titles (i.e. hand, hip, leg etc.) is obviously quite arbitrary for he did not use them in the rest of the *randori-no-kata* (i.e. *katame-no-kata*), and in any case they have no meaning as titles of throwing classes; what does hand-technique

---

* Kano himself personified this principle when he stood out against the pressure from the Japanese army to take over the Kodokan. By retaining his independence, by being there, staying as President, he could create moral force and so exert counter-pressure.

mean? Every throwing action uses the hands, so they must all be 'hand-techniques'. Another classic example of 'a name means an object, yet the object is not its meaning' is when *ukemi* is 'translated' as the 'art of falling over' and then promptly becomes a rigid style of falling down. If *ukemi* is to mean anything, it must mean simply that the body falls down – no specific way of falling, just falling as the Japanese ideograph conveys. In such a case the competitor should make the way of falling as compliant with his objectives of competition as possible – presumably that is to win. Therefore he learns a way of falling that does not automatically mean he loses (the competition), but allows him to avoid a terminal score so that he can continue with the contest.

It has already been suggested that a different *nage-no-kata* could be devised using two different sets of sub-titles for the naming of the groups. One would be stable and unstable techniques, and the other the principles illustrated in the *itsutsu-no-kata*. If the most is to be got from *kata* training the content of form must be infinite. There must be 'rays of infinite light' to show the performer how competitive skills can be varied.

When perusing any form of classification a healthy scepticism should always be applied. For example, take the instance of that very useful classification of general sport skills known as 'open' or 'closed'. In brief, the names refer to the amount of variables within a skilled performance; if there are many (e.g. football, tennis) it is an 'open' skill, if there are not many (e.g. golf, archery) it is 'closed'. It sometimes happens, however, that certain skills are difficult to classify in this way (e.g. judo throws) and in fact could be put in either category. Yet there is still a value in using these criteria, because the classification itself can be used to stimulate a different approach to the analysis of skills. For example, take any throw, put it into any category, quite arbitrarily – let us say 'open'; now what are the ingredients needed? Plenty of movement, many changes of body shape, plenty of pace variation – how does a competitor create those conditions? If he does not like open skills, but prefers closed skills, how does he convert an open skill to a closed one? As long as the classification is treated with flexibility it has value, but once it becomes sacrosanct its value diminishes to almost nothing. Therefore, if you want to get the most out of an open or closed skill classification, it may be better to ignore the physical situation of the opponent (whether he is stationary or not) and instead to decide by the personality characteristics of the attacker (see page 33).

Creativity

Creativity should play a major part in the 'open skills' of judo. To develop such skills, it is assumed, demands a great deal of creativity. So what is creativity? Many authorities avoid the question by taking the line that nominalism is the best policy. Perhaps it would be better if it were left so, but I like to start with a working definition, so that knowing where I have started, later on I shall know where I have been. However, I will compromise and only provide a general outline to encompass the area in which I shall be moving. Creativity must have something to do with art – the manipulation of reality. There will need to be curiosity and originality. Some authorities even add that self-actualisation is also necessary.§ Can it be separated from intelligence? Is it thinking and if so how can it differ from other kinds of thinking? Can there be a group creativity? Can a judo squad create a range of skills that is a monopoly of that group?§

There is a sophisticated type of classification that impinges on the profounder cognitive aspects of judo; it can be called 'field theory'.§ I want to use this theory as a starting point for a discussion on creativity in judo. The difficulty of comprehending what thinking, as a process, is, has already been mentioned. The difficulty is compounded when different thinking functions are contemplated. For example, how does creative thinking differ – in terms of mechanism – from 'ordinary' thinking? Field theory resulted from attempts to clarify different types of thinking. Through a long series of experiments (read the literature on creative thinking) two types or classes of cognitive processes were posited.

1. *Field dependent.* These were people who when given a complex visual schemata would see both the field (background) and the ground (the centre or focus of the schemata) with equal clarity and attention.
2. *Field independent.* These are people who when placed in the same visual situation can isolate – concentrate on – the ground and ignore the field.

Within these two polarities there are of course many disagreements and differences of opinion about the importance of the precise relationships of field to ground and how any differentiation is made, but the idea is straightforward enough. People do see life in fundamentally different ways, so can that axiom be projected any further?§ Does the way people view the world affect their degree of creativity?

Or does creativity mould the way they see the world? Does such an attitude of vision change during a life-span, or is it a pattern of thinking which is innate and permanent? To what extent, if any, is intelligence correlated with creativity? Must there be intelligence where there is creativity? Are they two separate processes, or just two sides of the coin of cognition? By using field theory as a speculative tool perhaps some attempt can be made to answer these many intriguing questions.

The many queries that arise from the relationship between these three items – creativity, intelligence, perception – can certainly be found in judo and any attempt to reconcile these three can affect training methods. Here are three questions whose answers will profoundly affect training. Are skills created? For there to be skill, must there be intelligence? Does the range of cognition determine skill? These are magnificent imponderables! But it is very exciting to try to sort them out. Let us discuss each query briefly, realising that many arguments are omitted and accepting there can be no finite conclusion.

Are skills creative?

If skill variation is to be ignored and everything treated simply as technique, the answer must be no. If the throws in the *nage-no-kata* are promulgated as rigid replicas of some original perfection, the answer must be no. If skills are to be 'hand-made' to fit each individual personally, and are an effective projection of that individual's personality, then it must be yes.

Zen, in talking about skill mastery to the aspiring performer, tells him that if he wants to be the master of the fight or the brush he must learn to encompass the whole sphere of action. There can be no focussing on details, like the position of the opponent's feet or hands, for that destroys the total comprehension which is an essential part of the top skill. The multiplicity must become one. Yet simultaneously it teaches that only by going through the needle-eye of death can that which is disruptive be transcended. Only by concentrating on the dot which is death can the freedom of selflessness be achieved.

Some of the investigators involved with the field theory began by trying to prove that creativity was linked with field dependence. Although there were some correlations, they found that some field independents could also be creative. Eventually they gave in and said that the 'true creator' would – and did – oscillate between the two types, thus getting the best from both (much the same conclusion as

Zen reached). It is another fine example of men trying to classify things and nature refusing to concede that there is any such thing as a class. As Gustav Mahler – a composer whose skill at mixing sadness and beauty produced a joy that surpassed the mix and became sublimely optimistic§ – wrote to his fiancée: 'You see, everyone who is going to live with me has to learn this. At such moments [when composing music] I do not belong to myself... There are terrible birth pangs, the creator of such a work has to suffer, before it all arranges itself and constructs itself and flares up in his head...'

Art, in the short view, is an interpretation of reality made by one person for the benefit of others. The nature of that reality will depend upon the perspective of observation, and that perspective can be modified by the degree of creativity within the individual. Can sport be art? Is judo art? Often the expression 'the art of judo' can be heard; is it just a nominalism or does it have any truth? In the way the statement is used, I would condemn it as nonsense. If 'interpreting reality' means an intention (by someone) to provide an unusual insight into and therefore a greater understanding of life, then judo – or indeed sport – has no overt design to do that. Its overt objectives are specific – to produce superior competitive performers – and have nothing to do with those of art. Judo may well have aspects which are aesthetic, movements which are delightful and made beautiful by their very utility, but beauty is not art.

Sartre suggested there are two intentions in the desire to play sport, that of 'to be' (exist) and 'to have' (appropriation). These two fundamental drives are used to create a particular form of reality (the game) in which the individual can so organise his own recognition as being.* It is here that there may be some contiguity with art, even an overlap, for art too can be – in the longer view – a creation of a 'new' reality, a reality in which the artist can identify himself. Andy Warhol paraphrased Descartes when he said, 'I paint, therefore I am recognised.' Therefore although it can be said that sport is not art in the sense that it does not start out with the intention of art – to offer a short cut to experience – it can end up by doing just that.§ For the spectator sport can offer short cuts to life-experience just as art does (perhaps some would argue at a lower level of inspiration, but an

---

* Perhaps everyone has, in some differing degree, the intention to create a 'personal reality' in which they can meaningfully exist. But some have the 'talent' to do it, others do not; some need little help from others to do it, while some need a great deal of help.

inspiration nevertheless), and to the participant also, sport can offer an unreal reality in which he can find himself, the same thing that art can do for the artist.

The effectiveness of his self-made reality for the individual sportsman or judo-player will depend upon his desire to create, and the intensity of that desire will depend to a greater or lesser extent upon the stimulation of the environment in which the individual finds himself; therefore if the most is to be made out of one's own personal reality (i.e. to become famous), the need will be to make the environment as exciting and as variable as possible. No-one wants to know a bore or a dullard!

For there to be skill must there be intelligence?

Of course this question begs the question, what is intelligence? An immediate clash with an insurmountable problem. No two people can seem to agree on a definition and the whole thing is exacerbated by that other provocative subject, I.Q. 'testing'. Do I.Q.s measure intelligence or simply the ability to respond to such tests? No matter, intelligence is not so much a thing, more a conformation to certain cultural expectations. As always, some people insist on classifying it; there are intelligent people who visualise a core intelligence (called 'g') which can cope with most things, aided by subordinate intelligence-units that handle special types of problems. Other intelligent people do not accept the concept of 'g' and see intelligence as a conglomeration of many specialist intelligence-units. Other groups, or perhaps it is the same groups, will argue heatedly as to how intelligence came to be intelligent. 'It is inherited', cry the innatists, but 'that's absurd', respond the constructivists; if it were true it would mean the single cell from which man evolved would have had the same intelligence as we do.§ Of course intelligence is a product of our environment, they cry; the innatists counter-attack by asking how is speech, beauty and justice brought about by an interaction with the weather? Toss up your prejudice and take your choice. Eventually of course both alternatives must be accepted or there will be another indistinguishable contradiction causing great confusion, but offering little insight.

Perhaps intelligence is the coping with knowledge; solipsism if the early stages of awareness — existentialism at a later stage. An intelligent person is one who seems to have a sensitivity to the needs of others, an empathy with the life around him, and an integrity of judgement that can distinguish the spurious from the sincere. Intelligence must also be something to do with that creativity which is concerned with the location of self within some form of life reality. A relationship between sport and art has already been looked for and it has been suggested there are conterminous areas where differentiation would be difficult to appreciate. But on the side of time there are axiomatic differences. Sport, particularly top sport, seems to have an insidious convergent effect upon participants (it narrows the outlook on life). They become egocentric. The training, because of its nature, tends to make them narcissistic, hypochondriacal, hyper-aware of the importance of self; there is no inducement for them to go beyond the confines of their own skill. Sartre's 'appropriation' becomes selfish indulgence and greed that are grossly physical. Skills fade away half-way through life, leaving the unprepared individual not only bereft of his original intention (that of being known in sport) but also destitute of any knowledge sufficient to initiate any other intention. Art, on the other hand, tends to have a divergent effect upon the individual (it broadens the outlook on life). The aspiring artist must study many subjects outside his own speciality: the painter anatomy, the musician sonics, the writer history, the sculptor engineering and so on. The artist can continue expanding and developing his skills well into old age and even to death. The dedicated artist acquires a generous attitude to life seldom found in a dedicated sportsman. Perhaps that is why Gombrich says, 'there may be no such thing as art, only artists'.§

Here may be a part of the solution to the query regarding skill and intelligence. The performer who does not allow himself to be sucked into the whirlpool of over-specialisation and sport for sport's sake (known in American colloquialism as the 'jock-trap') could be the one who is called intelligent. The one who allows himself to be exploited by the game, the officials, his own tunnel-vision, could be the stupid one.

Nevertheless the answer to the question 'does skill need intelligence?' must be no. It is of that same genre of questions that has haunted the moralists for centuries: 'does the artist need to be good?' 'does the creator of beauty need to be beautiful?'. Writers have enjoyed using this as a theme for many tantalising stories; Oscar Wilde's *The Picture of Dorian Gray*, Bernard Shaw's *The Doctor's Dilemma* and *Love among the Artists,* and recently Peter Shaffer's play *Amadeus,* are some well-known instances. The idealist says only the good can do good,* while the romantic claims that evil is the good done by the bad. The cynic says that good is done by those who find it easier than doing evil, whilst the realist claims that good is merely that which does least evil to the greatest number.

As for creativity, some writers have agreed that there can be four stages.§ They are:

1. *Preparation.* The complete immersion into the subject matter.
2. *Incubation.* The maturation of discovery among the lateral thinking processes.
3. *Illumination.* Seeing what should be done is understood.
4. *Verification.* Checking whether what has been done is what needed to be done.

The progress through these stages can vary in time. It may last a few weeks, or a few years, or a lifetime. The creator, be it of beauty, morality or sport skill, need have no integrity of action during the first three stages. If creativity were to stop there, there need be no relationship between personality and deed, i.e. a wicked man could produce a moral piece of art. But if the fourth stage had been reached and gone into then personality would have become an intrinsic part of skill and whatever was created would reflect that personality. An immoral man could only produce an immoral piece of art or sport skill.

So, if the most is to be made out of the individual's propensity to create, the intelligent player will look for the training that will stimulate him, and will seek out skills that will test his creativity. He will develop a curiosity that takes in more than just how to do *taiotoshi*. He will cultivate a passion – through the mastery of his own physical skills – for enjoying the skills and arts of others, not just among the ranks of sports people, but of masters of any skill. If the coach with whom the player finds himself cannot provide exciting training the player should find another coach. If that is not possible (perhaps the man is in the national squad and the coach is the squad coach) then the player must organise a player group to get the attitude of the coach changed. Sport must be a means to some other end than just winning; if it is not it is alienation of the worst kind.

Does the range of cognition determine skill?

Will his way of seeing life determine what sort of skills the

---

* It was for this reason that in my early days in judo we had to promise not to use judo for bad purposes; a form of oath-giving that is much out of favour today.

individual learns? In the above section on intelligence, it was suggested that the individual should make every effort to expand the purpose of training, if he felt it was too narrow. What if the individual wants to narrow everything much further and also knows precisely what all the implications are of that desire? The coach of course must respect those needs and if possible (and if it is compatible with the coach's own aims and objectives) satisfy them. In judo, as in other spheres of life, there are many who do not want to read books, who do not want to know what others have discovered; so be it – the race or the sport will have to find other people to lead life forward.

Tentative feelings in some of the investigations into the field-theory hypothesis suggest that field independents (those that can concentrate on narrow areas of attention) tend to be short on creativity.§ Such speculations are supported in practical judo. Those who do not want to expand their knowledge tend to cling to hackneyed skills and hence can be very boring to watch, because what they are doing has been seen so often. But if that is what they want, the coach should help them get it. Such encouragement to be like everybody else is easy enough if the coach himself is a convergent thinker. If he thinks that winning is everything, that there is nothing else but the skill, that there is no culture, no art worth wasting time on, then his task is an easy one. The great difficulty is when the coach is a divergent thinker.§ How does he cope with the convergent performer? Well, much more easily than the convergent coach with the divergent performer! It is easier for the ambitious coach to reduce his aspirations for the performer than it is for the hyper-specialist coach to broaden his range of interests for the ambitious performer.

One of the many problems with the convergent performer is his ever-reducing adherence to social and community responsibility. His training can become so insular, so self-centred, that he forgets he has any obligations to the community that supports him. He can easily become like some of the sportsmen in the 1980 Olympic affair. Then, it may be remembered that for international political reasons the democratically elected British government asked its sport representatives if they would join their government in making a protest against the Soviet Union by not going to the Olympic Games. Many sportspeople accepted the invitation of the government and joined its protest against international bullying. Many sportspeople ignored the request, not because they were in favour of international bullying or because they disagreed with their national government's protest, but because they had trained hard for more than a year and that – they said – gave them the right to perform in the Olympics. That right seems to have overridden the need to refer to any obligation they may have accrued while training. There is of course much talk these days about 'rights' – the right to work, the right to kill innocent people for some end that purports to be political – but seemingly with little realisation of what 'right' means. For the word is bandied about with no reference to its essential corollary of obligation. Rights are involved with relationships between two (or more) groups of people and if there are to be rights, both groups will need to make certain commitments to that relationship. The principle of fairness will need to apply to that relationship; each group will have to accept that it must contribute as much to the relationship as it expects to get from it, therefore if group A has an obligation to perform some service to group B, formed during a previous agreement by consent, necessitating a degree of mutual sacrifice of independence, group B has the right to expect that service; but equally group A has the right to expect a similar service from group B.§ As Hart wrote, 'When a number of persons conduct any joint enterprise according to rules and thus restrict their liberty, those who have submitted to those restrictions when required have a right to a similar submission from those who have benefitted by their submission.'§

Clearly the above, although being the most fundamental, but nevertheless the most essential, moral format between groups, can produce many complicated developments. Some moralists distinguish between natural and special rights; natural rights are those shared by everyone (i.e. the right to have justice), while special rights are those restricted to special groups. In this present discussion natural rights can be ignored and as for the special rights, they create special complications. For instance, what happens if the agreement of consent (as mentioned above) turns out to be unjust? Some writers will propose that it cancels the agreement, but many others will insist that it does not; the agreement must be adhered to, they say, if morality is to retain its stabilising position within society. The ruling consideration must be that the acceptance of benefits generates obligations and if in the context of a consent agreement a benefit is accepted, then so must the obligation.

The élite sportspeople did receive a considerable amount of assistance before the Olympic Games; large sums of money came from private and public sources (e.g. Sports Aid Foundation and government grants) and facilities and services were provided by various agencies (e.g. Sports Council and H.M. Forces). It could be said that the government's contribution was its recognition of an obligation to the sportspeople (some may complain it was not enough, but that – for the present – is irrelevant), therefore as well as giving the sportspeople the right to expect that service it could also be said to generate an obligation for the sportspeople. Yet I never heard anything of these obligations among the reasons given for going to the Olympic Games in 1980, much to my disappointment.

Here is the nub of the matter: the point at issue is not whether or not the sportspeople should or should not have gone to the Olympics, but the rationale they used to support the decision to go. What was the justification for ignoring the government's request and the obligation they had to it? It can be argued that any citizen must retain the (natural) right to disobey the state if the state demands an immoral service. In such an instance the individual will need to organise his reasons and if the state is just, those reasons will be taken into account when a judgement is made. Was the British government's request not to go the Olympics morally wicked? Many of those who did go to Moscow agreed with the government's sentiments regarding Afghanistan and agreed it should make some form of protest, but they thought it was unfair to ask them individually to join in that protest by not going to the Olympics. By seemingly ignoring their obligations to the state when composing their reasons for going, perhaps they were being unfair when they could only think of the 'training reason' for going? Why could they not have produced some moral support from their need to sustain a public or private obligation?

It was this kind of unawareness of civic responsibility that can develop in top sport which concerned Jigoro Kano and some of the other leaders of physical education in the early days of this century. This is why they were apprehensive of too much competition in sport, for something which begins small and insignificant can too often grow imperceptibly into a monster. This is also the concern of some contemporary sport educationalists. The place of sport is changing in society, from a recreational and physical form of education to a fanatical form of self-gratification; therefore its form of influence is changing too. Perhaps it is no longer benign and humanistic, but is becoming perfidious and making sport a corrosive factor in social morality. Perhaps the ideology represented by the slogan 'win at all costs' is more insidious than was imagined and is percolating into all aspects of sport and then into the community at large, deflating community values. Just as slavery insidiously undermined

Athenian civilisation,* perhaps perverted sport could undermine Western culture? For it should be remembered that it is not just society that moulds the morals of the individual; the individual in turn has a great effect upon society.

Of course, top sportspeople are the targets of many pressures that have little to do with excellence of performance. Since 1982, amateur athletes have been able to earn money by advertising and accept prize money. Such a change in official attitudes could make some sportspeople extremely rich, but their capability of earning such monies will depend on them winning and continuing to win. The temptation to 'cut corners' will be enormous. In fighting sports like judo, the results of 'cutting corners' could be much worse than in non-contact sports. A skilful and ruthless player who succumbed to such a temptation could, by actions undetectable by the contest officials, injure the opposition so that winning was easy. If such an attitude ever becomes acceptable to any degree judo could degenerate into a fight for survival.** In such an extreme instance training would become anti-social and that should not be the purpose of sport. We are back to Kano's intention: judo (and sport as a whole) should contribute to society, not detract from it. If sport is to teach aggression, as judo does, there should be strong compensatory elements that emphasise social obligations and responsibilities and teach the participants that their long-term task is to supplement culture, not destroy it.§

Many people both in and out of sport symbolically march under the banner of 'keep politics out of sport'. It is a strange cry. Politics have never been out of sport. If the Olympics are supposed to be taken as a *prima facie* case showing the purity of athletics, free from the 'dirt' of politics, what a bogus call it would be. Whether the classical Olympics of 776 B.C. to 261 A.D. or the modern Olympics from 1896, all would be the same; politics were an intrinsic part of all of them.§ And that's how it should be. If sport is to have any value, for either the individual or society, it must help train the individual to live in and

---

* One authority, J.B. Bury, attributes the despising of non-Greeks by Greeks as one source of a 'slavery attitude' that helped to destroy them.§ The same racial arrogance that was found in Hitler's Germany helped to destroy that country too. If ever sport ignores or despises the community that sustains it, the effect could be very similar.

** The film *Rollerball* showed what could happen to sport once such brutality was allowed to enter a game situation.

benefit from that society. That is what physical education is all about. Politics is an essential part of any society; how can it be ignored when any form of community training is being considered?*

Politics in sport comes in at two levels; first, the internal exploitation of sport; second, its external exploitation. The performer usually acquires some (small) empirical training in order to cope with the first, but virtually none for the second. Yet both types of politics will have major influences on how he plays the game. The enthusiastic performer may want to become an organiser when he finishes top participation; preparatory training would be of immense value to him during his training time. The élite sportsman should be very proud that now sport appears capable of influencing international standards of justice; why should he not learn how to use that influence to the best effect, both as a responsible citizen of a country and of the world? Art after all has always recognised itself as a political force, why not sport?

One of the reasons why some sport organisers want politics out of sport is so they can politicise more. If the participants became politically educated, the first people they would see through are the Machiavellian sports manipulators; they would be seen for what they are, exploiters from the inside of sport for their own selfish benefit. Such power-seekers never want the majority to become politically aware, for if they did those sports organisers would lose their positions. No wonder they want politics kept out of sport.

So – if the most is to be made out of morality in sport, let participation teach obligations, and training teach responsibilities to society.

Training

It may appear that if all the above were incorporated into a training programme there would be little time left over to teach the skills. That need not be the case. Top sportsmen spend many hours in training, much of it subsidised in one way or another. There are coaches or trainers who have the professional responsibility for organising and constructing those training schedules. Whether they intend it or not, they will inject their personal ideologies into those programmes; all that is needed, therefore, is to ensure that those ideologies benefit the greatest number – a kind of sporting

---

* It would seem evident to me therefore that political education should start within the school system.

Utilitarianism. A typical example of this kind of influence was found in the government's Centre of Sporting Excellence scheme, launched in 1975. It was based on the regions in the country and was the first real attempt to cater for sporting talent throughout the United Kingdom. Being the first of its kind it had, as is to be expected, many faults, but it did establish a pattern that others can improve upon. Probably its most important demonstrated proof was the need for highly trained coaches. The scheme recognised that its very existence demanded that performers had to be trained to the highest standards, but that could only happen if there were super coaches. Although there was a scheme for the performers, there was nothing for the coaches. The Centre of Sporting Excellence scheme showed very clearly, for those who had any doubts, that the key to the development of the right kind of sport in the future is to have a nationwide training scheme for the right kind of coaches—a scheme that would contain a curriculum roughly based on what has been outlined in this book.* Whether such a scheme ever materialises depends upon the creativity and the imagination of those who are responsible for structuring sport. It would be very exciting if judo could lead the way.

---

* A National Coaching Foundation was created in October 1982. It will be interesting to see how it develops.

Chapter 5
A Picture is Worth a Thousand Words

'He flourished the photograph: "There you are, that's the way to do it!" His friend looked surprised: "But that's not the way you teach it."
"Of course it is."
"No it's not! That bloke has got his elbow up and you say it must be down: his foot is there and you say it should be between his feet. It's totally different from the way you do it."
"Yeah, well . . . true I suppose." The photo-waver hesitated: " . . . but it's a good throw!"'

Some of the problems involved in looking at photographs have been mentioned in Chapter 1. There are a host of factors which it is essential to know if a judo skill is to be analysed in such a way as to help advise a performer how to improve his skill, but which just cannot be found in any still photograph. Here are the major ones:

1. What is the difference between the skill level of the two competitors? If the gap is a big one (and that can be true even if both are fighting in an international event), then the better man can do things to the other which he could never do to an opponent of his own ability.
2. What was the situation before the attack was made? Were they moving fast, slow or standing still? Were they moving in straight lines or curves? All would affect the decisions of the attacker – and the defender.
3. What happened after the instant of the photograph? What, if any, score did they achieve (see figs. 41, 42)? Did the target surrender as soon as the hit-man attacked, or did he fight him all the way into the ground?

Without having this information it is impossible to say if it is a 'good' attack or not. Indeed, what does 'good' mean? That it scores a terminal 10, or that it conforms to what the coach defines as good, or that it conforms to what tradition says is good? Presumably the ideal may be if all those criteria were applicable. Or if not, how many would make it 'good' – one, two or three, and which one of those three? If one criterion is not satisfied does that make it a 'bad' attack?

For me a good attack is concerned with the effective use of the individual's talents, the choosing of the right circumstances that will provide the individual with the best chance to utilise his trained, skilled elements to their best advantage. What more can be asked? If then it does not work, the 'fault' must lie with the opponent; he is too good!

Let's now look at a few examples of how techniques have been slightly or grossly modified by competitive circumstance. Sometimes the modification is made completely empirically, the performer not really knowing why he's changing it, only that what he learned before does not work now (fig. 45, I would guess, is one of those). At other times the performer knows precisely why he is modifying the technique (I would think fig. 27 is one of those). Sometimes the modification is made spontaneously, but as a result of a lot of training (fig. 15 would be one like that), while again others would have consciously changed it during training and assiduously practised that (fig. 40 would be one of those). As I said previously, I am not going to use traditional classifications when discussing these pictures, for that would just lead us into a certain type of expectation; I am going to use the simple heading of 'stable', both feet on the ground, or 'unstable', only one foot on the ground. A natural sub-heading will emerge – backwards and forwards – depending on the direction in which the opponent will be thrown. Ground-grappling is essentially all stable, but with slight exceptions (see figs. 46 and 47) while some throws seem to be stable in theory but not in practice and *vice-versa*. For example, body throws (i.e. *tomoenage*) appear to be stable, but are really unstable, while some 'trip throws' (i.e. *kouchi-gari*) appear very unstable, but are really stable. However, enough of this equivocation, let us start.

The stable group of throws
Both feet on the ground, but wide apart.

Fig. 1. A textbook *taiotoshi* technique. Tradition would emphasise the following teaching points:

1. The attacker's left leg is well bent, with the blocking right leg straight (so that I can generalise, the left leg is called the inside leg, i.e. inside the throwing arc, and the right leg is the blocking or sweeping leg.)

2. Because *taiotoshi* is officially a 'hand-throw', the hands are instrumental in pulling the opponent forward so that he falls over the blocking leg. The hands will therefore be pulling forward as near parallel with the ground as possible.

3. The attacker's body is as straight (up) as possible, with the bodies close but not actually touching.

Fig. 2. A real attack very close to the standard form. The attacker's body is bent rather too far to the side; unfortunately the hands cannot be seen, but otherwise it looks 'good'. However, the opponent has seemingly dropped his weight (by bending both his knees), making a throw very unlikely. No score.

Fig. 3 (below). Here the attacker is using the legs in the standard form, but is slamming his bottom and back hand against the opponent hoping that the leverage of his upper body will be enough to pull the opponent over the top. The fact that he is holding the opponent's left lapel instead of his left sleeve and that the bending of the right leg takes both bodies too far to the attacker's right, makes the scoring of 10 or 7 very unlikely. However, he may get a 5 or a 3 out of it.

Fig. 4. Much the same as fig. 3 but now this man gets the inside leg straight much earlier, which has the effect of getting the body weights more to the thrower's right. A high score is much more likely.

Fig. 5 (below left). Shows what appears to be a hopeless attacking position. The enormous gap between the bodies, the seemingly powerless position of the attacker, the left hand pulling down, would seem to add up to failure, yet...

Fig. 6 (below right). ... by straightening both legs, he certainly gets the opponent up in the air. However, he is falling backwards (look at number 15 on the ring-side) and that always points to loss of control. Because of the loose left hand the opponent will probably be able to get the right leg over and on the ground. If there is any score, I would guess 3 or 5 at most.

108 *Judo inside out*

Fig. 7. Here the attacker has both legs straight. The right hand pull is straight down, trying to pin the left shoulder of the opponent, so that he cannot step forward. There is a lot of space between the bodies, making control very difficult. The opponent has too much freedom about the head and shoulders. It will give him space to step over with his left foot. I would doubt if there will be any score, but if so it will only be 3 or 5, not more.

Fig. 8. The inside leg is straight, with the blocking leg bent. It shows that the weight (of the attacker) is well into the throw, giving the opponent little space to move in.

Fig. 9 (below). Is this a failed backward throw (*osoto*) or a failed forward one (*taiotoshi*)? We shall never know. Is the attacker thinking 'back' or 'forward'?

Comment

I prefer fig. 8. All the others need a great deal of flexibility, much of it not needed. In practice too much flexibility means a lack of control of the opponent's body. The flexible man zooms about but has little effect upon the opponent. Fig. 8 does not need flexibility but does require power to impose control on the opponent. For instance, for a throwing attack to have a good chance of success, the opponent's head should be lower than the attacker's.

Both feet still on the ground, but now close together

Fig. 10. A textbook *seoinage* technique. Tradition would emphasise the following teaching points:

1. Have both legs slightly bent, ready to straighten and so lift the opponent off the ground.

2. The attacker's right elbow should be under the opponent's right arm, ensuring lots of body contact, so that when the opponent has been lifted off the ground, the thrower bends forward and throws the opponent on to his back.

Fig. 17 (left). The thrusting left foot is a long way from the opponent. Both hands are pushing (if the right hand were pulling some part of the sleeve would be seen). The blocking leg is very low, around the Achilles tendon, and almost certainly is not sweeping/moving – because it would be blurred; it is just blocking. Direction of throw is over the opponent's left foot (opposite to tradition). It will be a middle score, 5 or 7.

Fig. 18 (right). Note the dynamic thrust of the left leg, again placed a long way from the opponent, driving the opponent backwards. Both hands are pushing. The right leg is very much just blocking and is as good as on the ground. Score 5 or 7, maybe 10.

Fig. 19 (below left). Both feet here are very much on the ground. The curve of the attacker's body would indicate that he is trying to throw the opponent over the right foot (traditional). There is no body thrust and hands appear to be doing very little. The body curve has allowed the opponent to get his weight on to his left foot. There will be no score.

Fig. 20 (below right). The traditional *kouchi*, the teaching points would be:

1. No weight commitment, attacker's left foot close to opponent.
2. Hand pulling forward.
3. Opponent's foot swept forward.
4. Direction – to the opponent's right back corner.

Fig. 21. There is the same body drive from a far-placed left foot as used in figs. 17-18. Hands are pushing, presumably the attacker's left hand is about to snatch the trouser leg to try to compensate for the fact that the attacker's blocking right foot has missed completely the opponent's right foot (an unintended mistake). The throwing direction would seem to be more over the opponent's left foot than right foot.

Comment

The practical factors seem to be fairly obvious here: the thrusting body weight, a blocking leg, not a sweeping leg (kept near the ground for safety's sake, i.e. difficult to counter). Direction of throw is over the foot that is *not* being blocked. Much the same as *ouchi*.

118 *Judo inside out*

The unstable group of throws: only one foot on the ground

Throws to the opponent's rear

Fig. 22. Shows a traditional *osoto*; the teaching points would be:
1. The three feet in line, as with both shoulders in line.
2. The attacker's weight is balanced on the left foot.
3. The sweep of the right leg would be from the hip.
4. Left hand pulls up, right hand pushes up.
5. Direction of throw—to opponent's right back corner.

Fig. 23 (facing page, right). This could have started somewhere near a traditional form. However, the hands are pulling or pushing down, the 'sweeping' leg is again only blocking and the hips are back (not forward). He may score 3.

Fig. 24 (left). The attacker's driving right leg is placed on the opponent's right side, giving great thrust. The left leg is hooked well in, holding the opponent's lower half still, whilst the upper body is pushed over it. Hands are probably being pulled down. A good score, 7 or 10.

Fig. 25 (right). Much the same as fig. 24; however, because the attacker has been careless and is holding the collar with his left hand, it has allowed the opponent to free his right arm. That will cost the attacker a few points, down from 7 or 10 to 3 or 5.

Fig. 26 (overleaf). A real 'grinder', this one. The attacker knows how important it is to get the head and shoulders of the opponent down, but has missed the head. He will be driving straight down through his right leg by bending his left leg. The opponent will be trying to 'sit' forward; he will probably give away a low score of 3 or 5.

Fig. 27 (below). Just like fig. 9, is this a successful *osoto* or a *taiotoshi* done in yet another different way? There will be a good score, 5 or 7.

Comment

Again the fundamental points that can be found in the most successful *osoto* attacks are: the placing of the driving foot near the opponent's foot that is *not being blocked*. This ensures that the drive is pushing the opponent over the outside edge of the blocked leg. Head control is important, the opponent's head should be pushed in the direction of the ground, straight down.

Fig. 28 (left). A traditional *kosoto;* note the following orthodox teaching points:
  1. The sweep is done on the sleeve side.
  2. The bodies are upright, little if any weight commitment.
  3. The sweep takes only one foot.

Fig. 29 (right). The competitive tension in the bodies has made it possible for both legs of the opponent to be taken from under him. Again, as there is no control of the arm, the opponent will use it to turn himself out of real trouble, resulting in what starts as a 10 score realising only a 5 score.

Fig. 30. This is a *kosoto* taken to an extreme form. The whole leg of the attacker has been used to sweep the whole leg of the opponent out from under him. Again control of the arms is poor so although there is enough altitude for a 10 score, the opponent will probably twist in the air and reduce it to 3 or 5.

Comment

It seems to me that over the past few years there has been a singular lack of appreciation of what the sleeve-grip is for. Many if not most are quite content to hold both the opponent's collars. Although this is good for defence it is very bad for attack, as these pictures show. The sleeve grip is to control the opponent's outside arm, so that he cannot use it to turn his body (whilst in the air) and reduce the score.

Fig. 30 may be a counter. It is the great horror of the one-legged attacker. If they are slightly off target the opponent will – quick as a flash – pick that leg out from under him and *pow*! what a landing. No wonder the majority of competitors prefer the two-legged throws. Here are a few more versions of the horrors:

Figs. 31-33 (below and overleaf). Show three progressively violent forms of the same simple, kick-away-the-leg-he's-standing-on counter. *Fig. 31:* the leg is hooked out from underneath him, score probably 3 or 5. *Fig. 32:* a kick, lift, turn and drop him on his

back, score 7 or 10. *Fig. 33:* Pick him up high, with the arm between the legs, kick the legs out from under him, turn and splatter him onto his back, score 7 or 10.

Comment

That is why it is important to know that in this type of attack there must be control of the opponent's head. If there is, countering is reduced to manageable proportions. But now let's look at those that work – well, almost.

Fig. 34. Here is traditional *uchimata*; the orthodox teaching points are:
 1. Left foot of attacker between opponent's feet.
 2. Right leg sweeping high, against top inner thigh of opponent's left leg.
 3. Right elbow kept low, hands push upwards.
 4. Direction of throw straight forward.

Fig. 35. A seemingly precise traditional *uchimata:* all the weight on the one foot, opponent lifted up clear of the sweeping leg, down for a score of 10.

I would guess there is a big gap in the ability of these two. The whole 'taste' is that it's too easy.

Fig. 36 (below). The attack has been good, but the opponent (who must have a lot of experience) has slipped forward, round the sweeping leg, and is now ready to counter. Notice that the attacker is driving straight forward, over all the toes of the left foot. It is nearly always a bad direction—look at figs. 38 and 39.

Fig. 37 (left). Another flat-roofed attack but this time with very little effect resulting. The opponent has 'sat' on the hips and held the attacker's weight in check. No score.

Fig. 38 (right). A good attack, notice that the thrower's weight is on the inside edge of the big toe – that's good. The body is rolling too much to the left. Again I would guess there is a big gap in skills here; an experienced performer would not let himself be rotated in this way (see fig. 37). A 10 score I am sure.

Fig. 39 (below). Must be a good one – at least 7. Again the thrower's weight is on the inside edge of the right foot, sweeping leg is high and the opponent is held in close with his head kept well down.

Fig. 40. Should be another 10, but the loss of the opponent's right sleeve will reduce that, certainly to 7, possibly to 5. Here the throwing action is very similar to fig. 15, showing that the hips are playing a much more dominant role here than in fig. 39. The low right leg would support that contention. There is a great thrust forward (from the *inside* of the left foot) and the opponent's head is lower than the attacker's, showing that there is an awareness of what is needed to achieve rotation.

Fig. 41 (below). This could be a good one, it has some of the signs (but not all of them). A good example of where a single picture could fool you; the opponent is off the ground, the relationship is strong, but . . .

Fig. 42. ... shows that the opponent has just gone straight up and straight down. Absolutely no score. Why? The gap between the bodies is too big, which has weakened the grip of the hands. The attacker's weight is on the little toe of his left foot – the outside edge (that is always wrong). The attacker is only going for lift, not for rotation: there must be both.

Comment

Rotation is always helped if the driving foot of the attacker is *outside* the base of the opponent. It means that immediately the opponent's feet are off the ground, rotation must begin to take place. The opponent's head must be somewhere near the front of the attacker's chest.

Fig. 43 (below). A traditional ankle-trip; the teaching points are:
1. The foot attached is on the same side as the sleeve hold.
2. It is a 'localised' action; only the leg is used, not the body weight.
3. The foot is being taken across the bodies, so making the opponent fall sideways.

Fig. 44 (left). It is difficult to see here who is attacking whom, but on inspection the attacker is on the left. He is trying to get body-weight into the action (by 'falling' backwards). His unusual two-sleeve grip gives this a little more credibility than if he were holding both collars, but it still does give the opponent a lot of space to move in and at the instant of photography he is trying desperately to step over the blocking foot. If he makes it he won't lose any points; if he does not, about 5 will be the result.

Fig. 45 (right). A successful attack, but the opponent will only sit down. At least the attacker is not falling back, but in his enthusiasm to get his weight forward he has lost control over the opponent's right sleeve and so cannot turn him onto his back.

Comment

There is a great flaw in the traditional form of this technique. It suggests that the attacker should use his blocking leg to stand on and his driving leg as the sweeping foot. A highly trained man will find this virtually impossible. Very few can change the 'natural' function of their legs (try jumping off your other leg–the one you don't usually use). This is the reason why even experienced players can lose control, as in fig. 45. The legs are not working as they usually work. If there is no grip on that opponent's left sleeve, there is little control and the score is bound to be low in spite of the 'good' throwing action. The attacker, if he throws this way, must turn more to his left as the opponent is falling. This will obviate the action of the free arm and keep the score high.

A Picture is Worth a Thousand Words 131

Figs. 46-47 (above). General grappling is by and large stable, gravity effect is minimal, thus allowing the competitor to depend entirely on his own body control. However, within that generality

there are relative degrees of instability. For example, fig. 46 shows the stable version of a popular pin (*kuzure-kamishihogatame*), but because of its stability the attacker has difficulty in moving quickly from one counter-move (a breakout) to another. It is no surprise that some competitors prefer the version in fig. 47, which is more unstable than fig. 46 but allows a greater flexibility in response to the opponent's attempts to break out of the pin. Again the choice is the competitor's.

Fig. 48 (above). A traditional straight-arm lock, *juji-gatame;* the teaching points would be:
1. Right foot in opponent's left armpit.
2. Opponent's elbow on thigh.

Fig. 49 (below). The orthodox 'foot in armpit' approach allows the opponent too much space, to spin in and so escape from the lock. The experienced competitor puts both legs across the opponent's body, which gives him greater control.

Fig. 50 (above). This picture shows what could be the start of a fig. 49 arm lock. If the man with his back nearest the ground can straighten his legs (which are already in position for the lock) he can knock the opponent over so that he falls onto his back, whereupon the attacker will end as in fig. 49. These arm locks can start from any peculiar position.

One last demonstration that unorthodoxy is frequently the mark of a skilful performer

Fig. 51 (below). Shows the famous 'stomach throw' *tomoenage*. The teaching points are briefly:
 1. The attacker drops straight back and rolls over.
 2. The foot goes into the opponent's stomach and pushes the opponent over.

Fig. 52 (above). Shows a fairly orthodox version in contest. However, the foot is not in the opponent's stomach, but on the top of the thigh (notice the foot between legs). What is weak is that the opponent has got so much air-space. Notice how he is virtually doing a headstand; it is quite simple for any individual with gymnastic ability to twist in this position and *not* land on his back. Probably there will be no score.

Fig. 53 (below). Shows a solution to this ever-present difficulty with orthodox *tomoenage*; the attacker throws the opponent *sideways*. Notice too how both feet are used to 'steer' the opponent sideways and onto his back. The opponent, because he is airborne for a much shorter period of time, has much less chance of twisting and avoiding what will certainly be a high score.

Conclusion

When I was selecting the above photographs, I looked through many hundreds in a session lasting about four hours. After about an hour or so I realised that there were only some three or four throwing pictures, and that these kept coming up, although with an infinite number of slightly different variations. There were a lot of stable throws, legs wide apart, legs together; quite a lot of back throws, almost as many pick-up-and-drop counters; a smaller number of unstable throws. Was that because that was all there was in judo competition? Or was it because – for some peculiar reason – they were the only action throws the cameraman liked taking? The camera-man assured me that it was the former.

If that is so it would appear that in competition, the stable throws outnumber the unstable by about 6 or 8 to 1. If that is true, perhaps it would be sensible to teach the throws in that proportion. For example, in introductory judo courses, the far greater proportion of time could be given over to teaching the stable throws. After all, those will be the ones they will be using in competition later, so why not make sure they really know them early? Why waste too much time on the others? If they, the novices, want at a later time to specialise in one-legged throws, they can learn them in 'their own time'.

Any attack in competition, at whatever level is being considered, is a compromise with existing conditions. No combination of circumstances will ever be ideal for an attack. The competitor will need to judge any particular combination of circumstances and then decide to go or not. Once having started he has got to be able to adapt to whatever turns out to be happening. He must be able to think his way through every attacking process. He must have a sound idea of what those circumstances can be and how they can affect his skills. In that way a picture may be worth a thousand words, provided that the words are rubbish and the picture keeps in touch with competitive reality. The competitor as well as the coach must be able to look at pictures with a sceptical eye and assess which part is a compromise with the instantaneous now and which is the result of long, hard learning.

Chapter 6
A Summing Up

'The judo Executive Council of six was in full session. It was an enthusiastic group. They all did judo: one was a bus driver, another a cat-breeder, then a butcher, a peripatetic judo instructor, a draughtsman and a shop-keeper. The bus driver/ treasurer was holding up the annual audited accounts: "We had a turnover last year of over £160,000, how about that?" All agreed that was good and then they turned their thoughts to the main item of the meeting – changes in the grading syllabus.'

Amongst the plethora of business management theories there is one that has a particular charm, both for its simplicity and its identification with how things are in the real world.§ It puts the development of business organisation in three main phases, and is therefore called 'Phase Development Theory', and it works like this:

1. *The Pioneer Phase.* Here is where it all starts. The leadership is charismatic and dynamic, individual flair is in great demand. Systems (if there are any) are flexible and adaptable to market needs. The Boss makes sure that the skills pursued are those that will improve marketing efficiency and further ensures that there is continual research to make the pursuance of these skills more and more effective. There is a 'family feeling' throughout the organisation and job flexibility is the rule not the exception.
2. *The Differentiation Phase.* Standardisation becomes all-important, bureaucracy dominates – flair and individuality are discouraged, pressure is brought to bear to bring everyone into line. The rule-book is supreme. Objectives become rigid and

---
§ When this mark is found, it means that there is a 'further reading' section in the bibliography.

inflexible, tasks are compartmentalised. The means become the end. Montesquieu in a different context puts it very succinctly: 'Government has two duties: one to give justice to its citizens, the other to stay in power. Unfortunately the second is always made more important than the first.'

3. *The Integration Phase.* Here the emphasis is on the social system, yet concern is still retained for skill development. Both organisational and human resources are integrated for the betterment of the whole organisation. There is a built-in readiness for change and a continuous re-thinking of attitudes and concepts, while decision-making is decentralised. Organisational teams are set up and they are encouraged to devise their own research projects and to see them through. Objectives are no longer singular but pluralistic; they are formed to match the different units within the organisation.

Judo in Britain has had something of this development experience. The middle of the 1950s was the beginning of the Pioneer Phase. The several charismatic 'Boss's' systems (when there were any) were flexible – to the point of confusion. Certainly the skills pursued varied considerably with each different Boss, each claiming to have the better way to success. By the late 1960s the crisis factors (indicating the end of a phase) began to appear, the reluctance to delegate (meaning loss of individual power), inter-personal and inter-group conflict, the urge to centralise. By the end of the 1970s the Differentiation Phase was well under way: standardisation in most things, individuality suppressed, bureaucracy ramming everything into compartments. Perhaps by the early 1980s the crisis factors for this phase are also apparent? Increase in size and complexity makes centralised control difficult; there is an upsurge in internal political exploitation, increasing competition from other organisations. Some of these are now evident. Will they augur the next phase? A part of the object of this book has been to show what that next phase could contain. Let the book be concluded by a summary of these new developments.

It would seem necessary to decentralise the decision-making process. Experimental and research teams could be set up in various parts of the country; the 'mix' would differ according to its purpose. In addition to the usual element of players and coaches, there would be doctors, sociologists, psychologists and sometimes even philosophers. Perhaps a 'players' union' would have a place; this would be a sub-organisation of players, within the overall structure, that could make the needs of the performer known. The management unit (to whom such teams or groups would be responsible) would not be of the authoritarian type as in Phase 2, but more of a co-ordinating unit. It would be responsible for ensuring that the teams worked towards a common goal; it would keep records of the teams' work and see that everyone was aware of what the others were doing. The management unit would maintain a central library of books and films etc. It would liaise with other organisations, both inside and outside Britain, working in the same field of development. It would set up a communications system that would allow membership and interested groups access to all this accumulated material.

Society needs a culture.§ It is needed as a depository for its accumulated experience, as a power source for its future thrust to fulfil its purposes. The educated person contributes to that culture; an ignorant one is a parasite on it.

Judo Inside Out has tried to show that judo is not just a series of techniques strung together to make up a competitive activity but a contribution to its own particular local culture. In the recent past judo has been treated as just a competitive sport, apart from the work of judo's founder Jigoro Kano.§ If, at any time, there were other purposes involved, they were mentioned only briefly in passing. In this book social interaction and community responsibility have been made out to be the most important part of judo training. Competitive skills are merely one of the means to that end, just as co-operative skills are another. Instead of making biomechanical problems the central factor in skill analysis, i.e. 'where do the arms and legs go?', as in the great number of judo text-books, here it is the ideological and conceptual problems that have been given the greatest importance; so let me finish with a few conceptual problems that have a particular fascination for me, and which if solved would, in my opinion, greatly affect training methodology.

1. *Linguistics.* How does language – words and phrases – mould and modify skills? We have mentioned how the form of the printed page has moulded thinking; is there a similar effect from the form of words on physical skills?§ When words are used by a coach under the impression that he is describing and transmitting a personal image of action from himself to a trainee, is anything at all like that happening? What the words could be doing (but totally unrealised by the coach) is eliciting images of

action in the mind of the trainee that are his and his only – nothing to do with the coach's. For any image can only be a projection of the recipient's own experience and therefore will be for ever much nearer to his own existing skills than to the coach's desired ones. Does that mean that the coach can never transfer his images? Does it mean that the coach can only coach what *he* can coach, just as the performer can only do what he can do? Certainly there may have to be learning of another person's language (probably the coach will have to learn rather than the performer) so that that person's language can be used by the transmitter.§ This may mean that words as such need not be used. If the trainee was very colour-sensitive (perhaps an artist), colours could be used: shades of red for shades of attack, blue for a front-attack, yellow for the flank; a musician could prefer sounds to represent action. Words of themselves can restrict skill-range: if they are parsimonious the actions they elicit will be mean and tiny; generous or even ostentatious, the actions will be likewise.

2. *Physiology.* To what extent is physiology a part of the thinking process? It is accepted that external stimulation can initiate chemical processes within the body – for example, stimulate the limbic system and there is aggression. Now any skilled performer knows that a skilled action with aggression is quite different from that same skilled action without aggression; put another way, they are different skills even though the intention is to be the same. Aggression is not therefore *added* to skill, it becomes an intrinsic factor, like strength.§ If that is so, why cannot other external stimuli initiate other intrinsic skill factors, for example the eye and hand co-ordination? If this were found to be true the next step would be how to simulate such stimuli in training. It would need much work by the coach; he would have to add yet another area of study to his already expanding range.

3. *Para-normal abilities.* Is a champion sportsperson the same as a good performer, only better? It has already been suggested that in some aspects, i.e. motivation,§ there is a drastic difference. In my experience such a drastic difference extends across virtually everything that contributes to his being a champion. The champion is not only different psychologically, but probably physiologically too, therefore it is no good the coach thinking he can teach the same things to a champion as he teaches to a good player—only more complicated. He may well need to re-design his whole approach to the champion.

4. *Energy.* Are there more effective ways of converting bodily intake to energy? Better energy utilisation? Are there other training methods which are yet to be found that would make energy utilisation its core element? The story of the little boy who lost 10p needs to be remembered. A man finding him searching in the cone of light cast by a street lamp asked him what he was looking for and where he had lost it. 'Tenpence, over there,' replied the lad. 'Why are you looking over here then?'–'There's more light here.'

Sport, like any other artefact of man, has no intrinsic moral quality. It is of itself neither good or bad, it is the purpose to which it is put that will decide its quality. Instead of looking at judo from the outside in, by looking at it from the inside out perhaps a different future for judo can be envisaged. It is to be hoped so, for it certainly needs one.

Glossary

Most words and concepts used are explained or defined in the text. However, there are a few that may need some further explanation.

Do
> (As in *judo, kendo, chado, zendo*.) Literally meaning 'way', both in the physical sense as in road or path and the figurative as in method or approach. It is related to *jitsu*, whose meaning can range from technique to creative crafts. *Do* is the way of using *jitsu*; it is concerned with the philosophy of how to create. *Do* is education, *jitsu* is performance.

Grappling
> 1. Vertical or standing grappling.
> This refers to the two competitors struggling for a tactical superiority. They are moving around, locked to each other by the hand-grips; relative positions change, body shapes alter; grips can change but contact is seldom broken.
> 2. Horizontal or ground grappling.
> The same as above, but both are now down on the ground struggling.
> The equivalent Japanese terms are *tachi* and *ne-waza*.
> *Waza* means act, a deed, a trick; *tachi* refers to standing up and *ne* is lying down. But rather than use words like 'standing trick' which sounds so feeble in English I prefer the word grappling. It is much more dynamic.

Ideograph
> (Or characters.) The Japanese language is written down with a modified form of the Chinese script (*kanji*). The Chinese, instead of devising a phonetic script (as in Europe), invented one that represented the idea or the concept. Its advantage is that it can be understood without being read; its disadvantage is the number of characters. As internationalism grows, ideography is growing fast in the West too. Seldom is there found on the door of a public lavatory a list of words–gentlemen, messieurs, Herren, etc. – just a simple ideograph. Numbers too are long-established, international ideographs. Meaning does not depend upon the sound but upon the composition.
>
> By joining two or more ideographs together a composite concept is formed, different from the single characters; therefore *judo* does not mean 'the way of ju', any more than 'football' means 'the player's foot the ball' (i.e. rugby football). Judo means what is in this book.

'Ji ta kyo ei'
> One of Kano's two famous maxims (the other is 'sei ryoku zen yo').

It means, 'by helping – improving – yourself, everybody – the community – benefits.' It is an attempt to encapsulate the social side of British Utilitarianism. It succinctly summarises Kano's views on judo's place in society. Certain Buddhist sects also contain elements of 'self-help' which allowed Kano to appeal to historical precedents if he wished to avoid overt allegiance to a foreign philosophy.

Jitsu
(As in *jujitsu*, *bijitsu*.) See *Do*.

Kano, Jigoro, 1860-1938
Professional educationalist, founder of judo. Born in Mikage some 100 miles from Tokyo. His family seem to have been of prosperous, middle class stock; as far as can be ascertained it was not of *samurai* origins. He had a great fondness for playing games and physical activity of all kinds, and apparently had a propensity for things English from an early age. Attended the Ikuei school where he specialised in English, entered Tokyo University in 1877 and graduated in English and politics in 1881. Appointed lecturer, then vice-principal of Gakushu In (The Peers School). Founded Kodokan judo in 1882. He was sent on a study tour of Europe 1889-1891. On his return he was made Council Member within the Civil Service and the principal of the Shihan School (specialising in English subjects). There was a great surge in judo theory around this time, and all the *katas* were devised. Appointed Japan's representative to the International Olympic Committee in 1909. From that time on there were two main directions in his life, very much parallel but also never quite touching. One was his professional career within the Civil Service and the other his amateur enthusiasm, judo. In the 1930s, struggling against the rising tide of fascism, he founded the Kodokan Cultural Association, an attempt to offset the worst of contest judo. By then judo had begun to spread in Europe, so in 1936 with the help of Messrs Takasaki and Kotani he visited Europe again. The purpose was to demonstrate his ideology of judo through his two assistants (both top judo performers) and his own lectures and talks. He died on the way back from an I.O.C. meeting held in Egypt.

Kata
A structured form of training, where a purpose is established to develop a particular skill or understanding, e.g. how to fight on the edge of the contest area. Most sports contain *kata* training of some kind; the equivalent names would be drills, skill-practices, pressure-training etc.

'Sei ryoku zen yo'
One of Kano's two famous maxims (the other is 'ji ta kyo ei'). Its meaning is, 'unselfish intent is right action'. It is an attempt to encapsulate the moral ingredient of British Utilitarianism. Right action is to do with morality and refers to the type of action that is good for the greater number. Intention is the power or the will to initiate action and unselfishness is concerned with obligation – to the community. So looking at the four ideographs as a whole, the meaning is that working for the betterment of the majority (everyone if possible) is the right way of working.

Tsukuri & kuzushi

An illustration used by Jigoro Kano (the founder of judo) to demonstrate that (human) dynamic power cannot be produced unless there is a firm base on the ground (Newton's 3rd Law of Motion). It is a principle fundamental in judo and Kano showed it by tilting a man till he was balancing precariously on a point on his foot, e.g. the little toe.

He then went on to demonstrate how a man thus posed is unable to produce dynamic power from such a position. To do that he must have his feet planted on a firm base.

Unfortunately it would appear that most British judo instructors have completely misunderstood the illustration, for the explanation found in most text-books is that the demonstrator shows a loss of control, which of course is just not true. What caused the initial confusion, here in Britain anyway, was when *tsukuri* was translated as 'breaking balance'. Having a man perched precariously on a toe does not mean he has no control, nor does it mean that he has lost his balance. He can certainly move from such a position as any dancer or gymnast will prove. What is happening is that the potential to produce power declines as the foot area in contact with the ground is less. It has little to do with balance or inability to move.

Tsukuri, meaning literally to manufacture – anything from building houses to growing flowers – in a judo context refers to building a throw, a technique or a skill, and that essential part of a skill, the preparation. What needs to be done, how has the attacker to prepare himself? What needs to be done to the opposition? All that is *tsukuri*; it has nothing to do with 'balance'. *Kuzushi* is what happens to the opposition as a result of *tsukuri*. It is the loss of initiative on his part, the loss of control – both of himself as an organised competitor and of the contest as a whole. Both, the opposition hopes, are very temporary, but the attacker once achieving *kuzushi* will try and maintain it as long as he can.

Warm-up

A series of exercises usually (but not necessarily) done at the start of the training/learning session, designed to prepare the trainee for the effort to come. Superficially it is for the benefit of the body, but essentially it is to prepare the mind to be alert and ready for any and every eventuality. Therefore warm-up should not be just physically stimulating, encompassing a wide range of movement (and it should do that) but should also contain stimulating and exciting elements that will make people think fast and comprehensively.

Too often, in judo training, warm-up is used simply as an excuse for the instructor to avoid having to plan skill-learning periods within the training period. The warm-up goes on far too long (I have seen it take up over half the available training time) and comprises such dreary and repetitive exercises that the minds become dull and stupid. Such a warm-up is completely counter-productive.

Notes and Bibliography

It has already been admitted that many top judo leaders do not like reading books, so they need not bother looking at the list below – but then I don't suppose they will have read this book anyway. For those who like a good read (and I know there are some of those as well), what follows is particularly for them. They are books which I have found very stimulating or relevant in spite of some other faults. They are by no means the only ones important in their respective areas, and no doubt the reader will be able to supply his own 'literary milestones'. The scatter is fairly wide, but then why not; is that not half the fun of reading?
The purpose of the book has meant that certain themes have become central and therefore have been touched upon in all or most chapters, but with a different emphasis; therefore it was considered unnecessary to refer books to particular chapters, but rather to subjects or themes. Books which are not connected to a particular theme are listed under the heading 'general'.

Book reading, when learning something like judo, has five purposes:
1. It consoles, in as much as it shows other people have made similar intellectual journeys.
2. It illuminates areas of knowledge that any one person has not the time or the ability to discover for himself.
3. It excites because it uncovers knowledge the reader did not think existed.
4. It helps to construct a scale of criteria, an analytical tool, by which other writing (and speech) can be assessed and criticised.
5. I personally get much pleasure from the way knowledge in one book interacts with that in another and thereby fires off new ways of looking at old ideas. Certainly I experienced this pleasure during my own postgraduate research (at the Polytechnic of North London). I have referred to it at various places throughout the book. The title of my thesis is 'Top performance in sport; an analysis of selected socio-psychological factors as found in specialist groups'.

Notes have been given to indicate very superficially the contents of books cited and how they relate to the theme. It may help you to choose which books to read.

GROUP-INTERACTION

This seems to be a neglected area within coaching know-how.

Berne, E. *Games People Play*, Penguin, 1968. An amusing but provocative approach to human relationships.

Brown, J.A.C. *The Social Psychology of Industry*, Penguin, 1973. Little has been written on the sociology of sport; in the meantime, therefore, the sociology of work has a distinct relevance.

Canetti, E. *Crowds and Power*, Penguin, 1960. Shows where 'group attitudes' can finish – in the big crowd.

Fox, A. *A Sociology of Work in Industry*, Macmillan, 1971.

Klein, J. *The Study of Groups*, Routledge & Kegan Paul, 1965. Discussion on skills within groups.

Simmel, G. *Conflict and the Web of Group Affiliations*, The Free Press, 1955. An early attempt to analyse conflict and its relation to competition.

Sprott, W.J.H. *Human Groups*, Penguin, 1973. A useful introduction to some ideas on group activity.

Tajfed, H. (ed.) *Differentation Between Social Groups*, Academic Press, 1978. Some interesting and different views on group relationships.

Tiger, L. *Men in Groups*, Nelson, 1969. Has an approach to the need for politics in sport.

LEARNING AND PSYCHOLOGY

Alderman, R.B. *Psychological Behaviour in Sport*, W.B. Saunders, 1974.

Deci, L. (ed.) *Intrinsic Motivation*, Plenum Press, 1975. A comprehensive overview.

Hearnshaw, L.S. *Cyril Burt, Psychologist*, Hodder & Stoughton, 1979. The dangers of having too much status.

Knapp, B. *Skill in Sport*. A long-established classic but still worth a read by any newcomer into the world of skill in sport.

McClelland, D.C. *The Achieving Society*, Van Nostrand, 1961. A standard piece on motivation.

McLeish, J., Matheson, W. and Park, J. *The Psychology of the Learning Group*, Hutchinson University Library, 1973. An overview of various learning theories.

Palmarini, M.P. (ed.) *Debate Between Chomsky and Piaget/Language & Learning*, Routledge & Kegan Paul, 1980. An exhilarating collection of opinions, theories, prejudices & knowledge. A first-class read.

Singer, R.N. *Coaching Athletics and Psychology*, McGraw-Hill, 1972. An account of character-factors in learning.

Tutko, T.A. and Richards, J.W. *Psychology of Coaching*, Alleyn & Bacon Inc., 1971. An analysis of coaches.

JAPAN AFTER THE RESTORATION

Bergamini, D. *Japan's Imperial Conspiracy*, Panther, 1972. A different and enthusiastic view of the battles within as well as without the national organisation that was Japan. It is long, but worth a few evenings' reading.

Halliday, J. *Political History of Japanese Capitalism*, Monthly Review Press, 1975. An opinion that Japan's spiritual strength was far more capable of war-winning than its economic strength.
Halliday, J. and McCormack, G. *Japanese Imperialism Today*, Pelican, 1973.
Moore, B. *Social Origins of Dictatorship & Democracy*, Penguin, 1969.
An excellent chapter on Japanese fascism.
Sansom, G. *The Western World & Japan*, Crescent Press, 1950. A 'must' for anyone interested in the subject.
Storry, R. *The Double Patriots*, Chatto & Windus, 1957. Includes a discussion on secret societies of which judo was a part.
Storry, R. *Japan and the Decline of the West in Asia 1894-1943*, Macmillan, 1979.

PERSONALITY

Claridge, G.S. *Personality and Arousal*, Pergamon Press, 1967.
An assessment of personality in terms of various categorisations.
Hardiman, K. 'The personality differences between top-class games-players and players of lesser ability' (M. Ed. thesis, University of Manchester, 1968).
Kane, J. 'Personality Research: the Current Controversy and implications for Sports Studies' in *Sport Psychology*, ed. W.F. Straub, Mouvement Publications, 1978.
Levine, R.A. *Culture, Behaviour and Personality*, Hutchinson, 1973.
A stimulating sweep over a wide field of personality and culture.
Maddi, S.R. *Personality Theories*, The Dorsey Press, 1976.
An excellent overview.
Maslow, H. *Motivation and Personality*, Harper & Row, 1970. An exposition of third-force psychology.
Vernon, P.E. *Personality Assessment*, Methuen, 1963. A review of various aspects of personality assessment.

WAR AND MILITARY WRITING

Bohannan, P. (ed.) *Law and Warfare*, The Natural History Press, 1967.
A primitive view of war by several anthropologists.
Bramson, L. and Goethals, G.W. (eds.) *War*, Basic Books Inc., 1968.
An anthology of sociological and anthropological studies of war.
Chandler, D. *The Campaigns of Napoleon*, Macmillan, 1966. An exhaustive description of many battles.
Clausewitz, Karl von, *On War*, ed. Leonard, R.A. and Howard M., Weidenfeld & Nicolson, 1967. A shortened version of the original.
De Beer, G. *Hannibal*, Thames & Hudson, 1974. A picturesque account of the great general and his tactics.
Fuller, J.F.C. *The Conduct of War*, Eyre & Spottiswoode, 1961.
Fuller, J.F.C. *The Decisive Battles of the Western World*, vols. I and II, Paladin, 1970.

Hart, A. *The Sword and the Pen*, Cassell, 1978. An anthology of historic writers on war.
Lamb, H. *Ghengis Khan*, Butterworth, 1928.
Montgomery of Alamein, *A History of Warfare*, Collins, 1968.
Sun Tsu, *The Art of War*, trans. S.B. Griffith, Clarendon Press, 1963. An excellent account of tactics – for any situation.

SPORT AND PSYCHIATRY

Atyeo, D. *Blood and Guts*, Paddington Press, 1979. Sport as anti-social.
Beisser, A.R. *The Madness in Sport*, Appleton Century Crofts, 1967. Sport is not all health-giving.
Berkowitz, L. *Aggression*, McGraw-Hill, 1962. A standard work on aggression.
Festinger, L. *A Theory of Dissonance*, Tavistock Publications, 1959. Do some people need conflict?
Holbrook, D. *Masks of Hate*, Pergamon Press, 1972. A schizoid culture produces a schizoid personality.
Marsh, P. *'Aggro'*, Dent, 1978.
Montagu, A. *The Nature of Human Aggression*, Oxford University Press, 1976. A comprehensive overview.
Selg, H. (ed.) *The Making of Human Aggression*, Quartet Books, 1971. A continental view of aggression.
Singer, J.L. *The Control of Aggression and Violence*, Academic Press, 1971. Does violent sport produce violent personalities?

THINKING

Blakemore, C. *Mechanics of the Mind*, Cambridge University Press, 1977. Wholly intriguing.
Bolton, M. *The Psychology of Thinking*, Methuen, 1972. A comprehensive introduction to the subject.
Cratty, B.J. *Physical Expression of Intelligence*, Prentice-Hall, 1972.
De Bono, E. *The Use of Lateral Thinking*, Jonathan Cape, 1967.
Intelligence: the Battle for the Mind: H.J. Eysenck *versus* Leon Kamin, Pan Books, 1981.
Nagel, T. 'Brain Bisection and the Unity of Consciousness', from *The Philosophy of Mind*, ed. J. Glover, Oxford University Press, 1980.
Rose, S. *The Conscious Brain*, Weidenfeld & Nicolson, 1973. Just as intriguing as Blakemore.
Ryle, G. *The Concept of Mind*, Penguin, 1978. A 'must' for any judo thinker.
Vanck, M. and Cratty, B.J. *Psychology and the Superior Athlete*, Macmillan, 1970.

ZEN AND SKILLS

There are many books, but here are a few that I found particularly stimulating:
Ando, S. *O Yo Mei no Kaidakkan*, Shobun Kan, 1943 (Japanese). 'Oyomei' is the Japanese pronunciation of Wang Yang Ming. His book attempts to show how the teachings can apply to wartime Japan.

Blyth, R.H. *Zen in English Literature and Oriental Classics*, Hokuseido Press, 1942. All of Blyth's books are excellent.
Capleau, P. (ed.) *Three Pillars of Zen*, Harper & Row, 1966. A western view of Zen; it is different.
Herrigel, E. *Zen and the Art of Archery*, Routledge & Kegan Paul, 1953. Has now become a classic of Japanese obfuscation.
Kammer, R. *Zen and Confucius in the Art of Swordsmanship*, Routledge & Kegan Paul, 1978.
Mishima, Y. *On Hagakure*, Penguin, 1977. It does of course only contain pieces of *Hagakure*; a full text can only be found in Japanese.
Nakuriya, K. *The Religion of the Samurai*, Luzac, 1913. An excellent account of Zen as related to the fighting men.
Suzuki, D.T. *Zen and its Influence on Japanese Culture*, Routledge & Kegan Paul, 1959. The correspondence between Takuan and Yagyu Tajima no kami Munenori are of particular interest to skill-developers.
Suzuki, D.T. and Fromm, E. *Zen Buddhism and Psychoanalysis*, Condor Books, 1960.

EDUCATION, THEORY AND IDEOLOGY

Adams, J. *Modern Development in Educational Practice*, University of London Press, 1922. A past perspective on education.
Bantock, G.H. *Freedom and Authority in Education*, Faber & Faber, 1952. A liberal view of education.
Chart, C. and Fawd, J. (eds.) *Darwin to Einstein*, Longmans, 1980. An American educational approach to Pareto (the élitist).
Evans, K. *The Development and Structure of the English Educational System*, University of London Press, 1975.
Gruber, H.E. Voneche (ed), *The Essential Piaget*, Routledge & Kegan Paul, 1977. 'The Semiotic and Symbolic Function', pp. 483 - 507.
Herron, R.E. and Sutton-Smith, B. *Child's Play*, J. Wiley & Sons Inc., 1971. The role of play in child development.
Nettleship, R.L. *The Theory of Education in Plato's Republic*, Oxford University Press, 1935. The chapter on 'Music and Gymnastics' is very relevant to sports training.
Peters, R.S. (ed.) *The Concept of Education*, Routledge & Kegan Paul, 1967. A very useful chapter by G. Ryle.

LEISURE, SOCIOLOGY AND SPORT

Crocker, L.G. *Nature and Culture*, Johns Hopkins University Press, 1963. A Utilitarian view of sport.
Dumazedier, J. *The Sociology of Leisure*, Elsevier, 1974. A French view which, because of its difference, makes many stimulating points.
Keck, A.J. (ed.) *Selected Writings of G.H. Mead*, University of Chicago Press, 1964. Has much to say to a coach.
Linder, S.B. *The Harried Leisure Class*, Columbia University, 1970. A Swede's view, an excellent sequence of mental shocks.

Mumford, L. *The Myths of the Machine*, Secker & Warburg, 1967.
A fascinating read, full of ideas and mental 'time bombs'.
Smith, M., Parker, S. and Smith, C. (eds.) *Leisure and Society in Britain*, Allen Lane, 1973. A home view.
Riordan, J. *Soviet Sport*, Blackwell, 1980.
Riordan, J. *Sport under Communism*, C. Hurst, 1978. Any book by Riordan is good reading.
Wilson, E.O. *Sociobiology*, Beldrop Press, 1975. Another big read, but worth every hour.
Sport Sociology. The Annals of the American Academy of Political & Social Science, September 1979.

PHILOSOPHY AND SPORT

Afuan, R. *Zoroaster's Influence on Greek Thought*, Philosophical Library Inc., New York, 1965. Another form of Form.
Best, D. *Philosophy and Human Movement*, Allen & Unwin, 1978. Excellent reading.
Coppleston, F. *A History of Philosophy*, vol. VIII, parts 1 and 2, Image Books, 1967. A comprehensive view and one easy to read of the impact of Utilitarianism on Britain and America.
Fletcher, R. (ed.) *John Stuart Mill*, Nelson, 1971. A comprehensive overview of Mill's work. Very good.
Hall, S. and Jefferson, T. (eds.) *Resistance through Ritual*, Hutchinson University Library, 1976. The growth of sub-cultures.
Hayek, F.A. *New Studies*, Routledge & Kegan Paul, 1978. Seems to have an affinity with Kano.
Hyman, A. and Walsh, J.J. (eds.) *Philosophy in the Middle Ages*, Hacket Publishing Co., 1977. A good place to start looking for the mind and body relationship.
Mikhailov, F.T. *The Riddle of the Self*, Progress Publishers, Moscow, 1976. An unexpected view of the Self from a Russian standpoint.
Needham, J. *Science and Civilisation in China*, vol. II, Cambridge University Press, 1956. Read Chapter 16.
Popper, K. *The Open Society and its Enemies*, vol. I, Routledge & Kegan Paul, 1945. His criticism of Plato and his Form.
Sartre, J.P. *Being and Nothingness*, Methuen, 1943. Very heavy going but section on 'Doing and Having', pp. 575 - 90, is worth trying.
Scharfstein, B.A. *The Philosophies*, Basil Blackwell, 1980. How do philosophers philosophise? Could it refer to sportsmen too?
Slusher, A.S. *Man, Sport and Existence*, H. Kimpton, 1967. An exasperating writer, but he provokes thought.
Teilhard de Chardin, P. *The Phenomena of Man*, Fontana Books, 1955. Again it is exciting to relate him to Mikhailov.
Weiss, P. *Sport, a Philosophic Enquiry*, S. Illinois University Press, 1969. Tries to explain why there is so little written on the philosophy of sport.

ART AND CREATIVITY

Ehrenzweig, A. *The Hidden Order of Art*, Paladin, 1970. A fascinating approach to what is art – and therefore coaching.

Gombrich, E.H. *Art and Illusion*, Phaidon Press, 1959. *Meditations on a Hobby Horse*, Phaidon Press, 1963. Excellent books for any coach to read.

Lamb, W. *Posture and Gesture*, Duckworth, 1965. An attempt to relate demonstration to personality.

Rosenberg, H. *Art on the Edge*, Secker & Warburg, 1976. A very sound commentary on contemporary theories.

Taylor, R.L. *Art, an Enemy of the People*, Harvester Press, 1978. He could try the same arguments on sport.

Vernon, P.E. (ed.), *Creativity*, Penguin, 1975.

MORALITY AND FAIR PLAY

McIntosh, P. *Fair Play*, Heinemann, 1979. An excellent account of morality in sport – is there any?

Moore, G.E. *Principia Ethica*, Cambridge University Press, 1959.

Rawls, J. *A Theory of Justice*, Oxford University Press, 1971. Massive, but it analyses most possible situations.

Sidgwick, H. *History of Ethics*, Macmillan, 1967. An overview of the history of ethics.

Simmons, A.J. *Moral Principles and Political Obligations*, Princeton University Press, 1979. A much shorter run over much the same ground as Rawls.

N.B. The emphasis here in both philosophy and morality is on Utilitarianism because that is where much of Kano's thought was founded.

BUSINESS ORGANISATION

Etzioni, A. *Modern Organisation*, Prentice-Hall, 1964. An excellent view of the American scene.

Handy, C.B. *Understanding Organisations*, Penguin, 1976. A comprehensive view of organisations.

Jay, A. *Management and Machiavelli*, Pelican, 1970. A different view of management, using history as a trigger. The theory of organisation is seldom found in sport; it well deserves a place.

Kahn, R.L. *Organisational Stress*, Wiley, 1964. Here conflict in management relations is used as a means of achieving efficiency.

McGregor, D.M. *Adventures in Thought and Action*. Proceedings of the Fifth Anniversary Convocation of the School of Industrial Management, Massachusetts Institute of Technology, 1957. A different view of work motivation. It is stimulating and could apply to sport.

Mills, C.W. *Power, Politics and People*, Oxford University Press, 1963. A collection of essays that are very enjoyable, from discussion on the Chinese language through work and leisure to competition.

Schon, D.A. *Beyond the Stable State*, M. Temple-Smith, 1971. Public and private learning in a changing society. An exciting view of what organisation could do.

Tannenbaum, A.S. *Social Psychology of the Work Organisation*, Wadsworth, 1966.

GENERAL

Barnett, P.M. *Judo to Win*, United States Judo Association, 1973.

Barnett, P.M. *Judo Groundplay to Win*, United States Judo Association, 1974. The author is British, but his views were too *avant garde* for British publishers. Both excellent books.

Blaukopf, K. *Mahler*, Futura Publications, 1974.

Brecht, B. *The Life of Galileo*, Methuen, 1980.

Bury, J.B. *A History of Greece*, The Modern Library, 1913. A standard book for classical Greece.

Finely, M.M.I. and Pleket, H.W. *The Olympic Games*, Chatto & Windus, 1976. An excellent account of the classic Games.

Halliday, J. and Fuller, P. *The Psychology of Gambling*, Penguin, 1977. Several pieces showing different manifestations of gambling.

Jigoro Kano, *A biography*, Kodokan Japan, 1965. Again, unfortunately, only in Japanese.

Koizumi, G. *My Study of Judo*, Foulsham, 1960. It could almost be called 'A study of my judo'; it gives an excellent account of judo as seen by someone just after the Second World War.

McLuhan, M. *The Gutenberg Galaxy*, Routledge & Kegan Paul, 1962. The impact of the printed page on thinking.

Macluire, J.S. *Educational Documents*, Methuen, 1965. An account of most Education Acts between 1816 and 1967?

Nakamura, T. *Supotsu to wa nanika*, Popura Bukkusu, 1974. Unfortunately for most readers, this is in Japanese; however, it talks very interestingly about how Japanese see sport.

Popper, K. 'The Science of Galileo and its new Betrayal', from *Conjectures and Refutations*, Routledge & Kegan Paul, 1963. Popper is always good for a think and relating him to Brecht is good fun.

Voltaire. *Candide*, Dr Pangloss was the arch-optimist – 'all is for the best in the best of all possible worlds'.

Index

Japanese and British technical terms

Ashiguruma, 44, 45, 88
Balance, break *(tsukuri* and *kuzushi)*, 51-52, 144
Body contact, 60
Combination attacks, 46
Countering principles, 42ff., 50
Dojo, 75
Falling down *(ukemi)*, 13, 55, 57, 58, 90
Feet, use of, 59
Foot trips, 25, 26, 29, 104, 129
Go-no-sen, 46
Hands, use of, 59
Hanegoshi, 29
Haraigoshi, 29, 88
Harai-tsurikomi-ashi, 49
Hizaguruma, 88
Itsutsu-no-kata, 87, 89, 90; principles of, 88
Ju/Go-no-kata, 86
Juji-gatame, 27, 47, 132; skill of, 28; variations, 27
Kata, 25, 35, 66, 68, 85, 86, 88, 89, 90, 143
Katame-no-kata, 89
Katame-waza, 29, 30
Kiai, 52
Kosoto, 26, 44, 121
Kouchi, 44, 46, 88, 89, 104, 116
Kuzure-kami-shihogatame, 23, 131
Nage-no-kata, 35, 89, 90, 92
Ne-waza, 23, 24, 47, 51
Opportunity, 26, 60, 81, 82, 83
Osaekomi, 30
Osoto, 22, 23, 44, 45, 46, 52, 118; variations, 23;

osotogaeshi, 88
Ouchi, 51, 62, 68, 114
Randori, 66
Randori-no-kata, 25, 89
Renraku-waza (linked attacks), 46, 88
Seoinage, 26, 44, 52, 88, 89, 110; *ippon*, 26, 47; variations, 27
Shiai, 61
Shobu, 61
Strangles, 30
Sutemi-waza, 29, 88
Tactics, 22, 29, 31, 32, 34, 37, 54, 56, 58, 67, 68
Taiotoshi, 22, 45, 46, 57, 68, 88, 89, 96, 105
Technique, 15, 19, 20, 25, 30, 104, 139; definition, 20, 56
Tokui-waza, 37
Tomoenage, 104, 133
Tsurikomigoshi, 46
Uchikomi, 79, 83, 84; *Uchikomi*-on-the-move, 85
Uchimata, 88
Weight, use of, 59
Yoko-shihogatame, 47

Subjects

Aesthetics, 64
Aggression, 22, 140
Art, 65, 91, 93, 94, 95, 96, 101; artist, 65, 94, 95
Ballistic movement, 29, 82
Beauty, 65
Boredom, 48

Brain bisection, 81
British government, 97
Centres of (Sport) Excellence Scheme, 102
Champion(s), 34, 48, 53, 54, 82, 140
China, 86
Classification, 89, 90, 94;
  dangers of, 28, 29, 30
Coach, responsibilities of, 69, 70, 71, 101;
  qualities of, 70, 104;
  attitudes of, 34, 35, 74, 76, 78, 96, 97, 135, 139, 140;
  definition of, 69
Competition, 65, 66, 67;
  attitudes to, 21;
  rules of, 31, 37;
  scores in, 57, 58, 68
Creativity, 33, 91, 92, 96
Culture, effects of, 33, 64, 65, 87, 100, 139
Curiosity, 48, 74, 75, 76, 91
Energy, 141
Field theory, 91, 92, 97
Form and content, 32, 35;
  form, 32, 43, 86, 88
Gakushu In (the Peers Schools), 87
Gambling, 29
Gamesmanship, 76
Gestalt, 35, 36
Grading syllabus, 19, 24, 61
Groups, 15, 98;
  judo groups, 14, 25, 76, 77, 78, 91, 95;
  group learning, 14, 20, 68
Hagakure, 83, 84
Innate ability, 56, 64, 94
Inner sport, 79
Intelligence, 92, 94, 95, 96
Introduction Course (Beginners' Course), 19, 25, 56, 60, 61, 67, 68, 69, 135
Japanese army, 31, 66, 89n.
Kodokan, 75
Learning, 14, 19, 27, 35, 43, 47, 48, 66
Linguistics, 139
Military writings, 37, 38, 50

Motivation, 33, 36, 62, 76, 77, 78, 140;
  lack of, 54
Movement, quality of, 22, 56, 62, 63, 64, 65;
  pattern of, 67
National coaching institution, 71
National squads, 76
Olympic Games, 97, 98, 99, 100
Para-normal abilities, 140
Personality, sport, 32, 33, 35, 43, 53, 64
Phase Development Theory, 137
Photographs, 15, 30, 31, 103
Physical education, 66, 99, 101
Physiology, 140
Politics, 38, 39, 71, 74, 100, 101
Psychiatric problems, 34
Psychology of sport, 73
Responsibility, social, 70, 99, 101, 139
Rights (morals/ethics), 70, 76, 141
Ritual, 84
Samurai, 31, 83, 84
Self-defence, 66
Skill, 19, 20, 29, 35, 36, 47, 48, 56, 57, 65, 67, 68, 77, 82, 83, 84, 92, 95, 101, 138;
  definition of, 20, 21;
  fashion, 30;
  open and closed, 90, 91
Soviet Union, 97
Sports Council, 98
Stability (as a criterion of analysis), 29
Tao, 86
Teaching methodology, 53, 55
Thinking, 79, 80, 81, 82, 91, 135, 140
Training programme, 30, 66, 75, 101;
  social, 66
War, 38, 39
Yin-yang logogram, 78, 79, 81, 86
Zen Buddhism, 36, 78, 83, 92, 93

Names

Chomsky, Noam, 53
Clausewitz, Karl Maria von, 38
De Bono, Edward, 82n.
Galileo, 74
Gombrich, Ernst H., 95
Kano, Jigoro, 14, 29, 31, 66, 67, 75, 86, 87, 88, 89, 99, 100, 139, 143;
  trip to Europe, 87
Mahler, Gustav, 93
Mill, John Stuart, 75, 79, 86, 87
Mishima, Yukio, 83
Montesquieu, 139
Nagel, Thomas, 81
Piaget, Jean, 53
Plato, 85, 86
Popper, Karl R., 85, 89
Raphael, 35, 48
Ryle, Gilbert, 80
Sartre, Jean-Paul, 36, 53, 77, 93, 95
Shao Yung, 86
Spencer, Herbert, 66, 75, 86
Socrates, 78
Teilhard de Chardin, Pierre, 53
Wittgenstein, Ludwig, 81
Warhol, Andy, 93
Zoroaster, 85

DANIEL O'DONNELL

Notable dates 2011

January

1	Saturday	New Year's Day
3	Monday	Holiday (UK, R of Ireland, AUS, NZL)
4	Tuesday	Holiday (NZL, SCT)
17	Monday	Martin Luther King, Jr. Day (Holiday USA)
25	Tuesday	Burns Night (SCT)
26	Wednesday	Australia Day (Holiday AUS)

February

6	Sunday	Waitangi Day (Holiday NZL)
14	Monday	St Valentine's Day
21	Monday	Washington's Birthday (Holiday USA)

March

1	Tuesday	St David's Day
8	Tuesday	Shrove Tuesday
13	Sunday	Daylight Saving Time begins (CAN, USA)
14	Monday	Commonwealth Day
17	Thursday	St Patrick's Day (Holiday R of Ireland, N Ireland)
27	Sunday	British Summer Time begins European Daylight Saving Time begins

April

3	Sunday	Mother's Day (UK, Ireland) Daylight Saving Time ends (NZL, AUS - except WA, NT, QLD)
22	Friday	Good Friday (Holiday UK, AUS, CAN, NZL) Earth Day
23	Saturday	St George's Day
24	Sunday	Easter Sunday
25	Monday	Easter Monday (Holiday UK except SCT, R of Ireland, AUS, NZL) Anzac Day

May

2	Monday	Holiday (UK, R of Ireland)
8	Sunday	Mother's Day (AUS, CAN, NZL, USA)
23	Monday	Victoria Day (Holiday CAN)
30	Monday	Holiday (UK) Memorial Day (Holiday USA)

June

6	Monday	Queen's Birthday (Holiday NZL) Holiday (R of Ireland)
19	Sunday	Father's Day (UK, CAN, USA)

July

1	Friday	Canada Day (Holiday CAN)
4	Monday	Independence Day (Holiday USA)
12	Tuesday	Battle of the Boyne (Holiday N Ireland)

August

1	Monday	Holiday (Scotland, R of Ireland)
29	Monday	Holiday (UK except SCT)

September

4	Sunday	Father's Day (AUS, NZL)
5	Monday	Labor Day (Holiday USA)
		Labour Day (Holiday CAN)
21	Wednesday	UN International Day of Peace
25	Sunday	Daylight Saving Time begins (NZL)

October

2	Sunday	Daylight Saving Time begins (AUS - except WA, NT, QLD)
4	Tuesday	World Animal Day
10	Monday	Columbus Day (Holiday USA)
		Thanksgiving Day (Holiday CAN)
24	Monday	Labour Day (Holiday N7L)
30	Sunday	British Summer Time ends
		European Daylight Saving time ends
31	Monday	Holiday (R of Ireland)
		Hallowe'en

November

5	Saturday	Bonfire Night
6	Sunday	Daylight Saving Time ends (CAN, USA)
11	Friday	Veterans' Day (Holiday USA)
		Remembrance Day (Holiday CAN)
13	Sunday	Remembrance Sunday (UK)
24	Thursday	Thanksgiving Day (Holiday USA)
30	Wednesday	St Andrew's Day (Holiday SCT)

December

24	Saturday	Christmas Eve
25	Sunday	Christmas Day
26	Monday	Boxing Day
		(Holiday UK, USA, CAN, AUS, NZL)
27	Tuesday	Holiday (UK, AUS, NZL, CAN)
31	Saturday	New Year's Eve

2011

JANUARY
M	T	W	T	F	S	S
31					1	2
3	4	5	6	7	8	9
10	11	12	13	14	15	16
17	18	19	20	21	22	23
24	25	26	27	28	29	30

FEBRUARY
M	T	W	T	F	S	S
	1	2	3	4	5	6
7	8	9	10	11	12	13
14	15	16	17	18	19	20
21	22	23	24	25	26	27
28						

MARCH
M	T	W	T	F	S	S
	1	2	3	4	5	6
7	8	9	10	11	12	13
14	15	16	17	18	19	20
21	22	23	24	25	26	27
28	29	30	31			

APRIL
M	T	W	T	F	S	S
				1	2	3
4	5	6	7	8	9	10
11	12	13	14	15	16	17
18	19	20	21	22	23	24
25	26	27	28	29	30	

MAY
M	T	W	T	F	S	S
30	31					1
2	3	4	5	6	7	8
9	10	11	12	13	14	15
16	17	18	19	20	21	22
23	24	25	26	27	28	29

JUNE
M	T	W	T	F	S	S
		1	2	3	4	5
6	7	8	9	10	11	12
13	14	15	16	17	18	19
20	21	22	23	24	25	26
27	28	29	30			

JULY
M	T	W	T	F	S	S
				1	2	3
4	5	6	7	8	9	10
11	12	13	14	15	16	17
18	19	20	21	22	23	24
25	26	27	28	29	30	31

AUGUST
M	T	W	T	F	S	S
1	2	3	4	5	6	7
8	9	10	11	12	13	14
15	16	17	18	19	20	21
22	23	24	25	26	27	28
29	30	31				

SEPTEMBER
M	T	W	T	F	S	S
			1	2	3	4
5	6	7	8	9	10	11
12	13	14	15	16	17	18
19	20	21	22	23	24	25
26	27	28	29	30		

OCTOBER
M	T	W	T	F	S	S
31					1	2
3	4	5	6	7	8	9
10	11	12	13	14	15	16
17	18	19	20	21	22	23
24	25	26	27	28	29	30

NOVEMBER
M	T	W	T	F	S	S
	1	2	3	4	5	6
7	8	9	10	11	12	13
14	15	16	17	18	19	20
21	22	23	24	25	26	27
28	29	30				

DECEMBER
M	T	W	T	F	S	S
			1	2	3	4
5	6	7	8	9	10	11
12	13	14	15	16	17	18
19	20	21	22	23	24	25
26	27	28	29	30	31	

2012

JANUARY
M	T	W	T	F	S	S
30	31					1
2	3	4	5	6	7	8
9	10	11	12	13	14	15
16	17	18	19	20	21	22
23	24	25	26	27	28	29

FEBRUARY
M	T	W	T	F	S	S
		1	2	3	4	5
6	7	8	9	10	11	12
13	14	15	16	17	18	19
20	21	22	23	24	25	26
27	28	29				

MARCH
M	T	W	T	F	S	S
			1	2	3	4
5	6	7	8	9	10	11
12	13	14	15	16	17	18
19	20	21	22	23	24	25
26	27	28	29	30	31	

APRIL
M	T	W	T	F	S	S
30						1
2	3	4	5	6	7	8
9	10	11	12	13	14	15
16	17	18	19	20	21	22
23	24	25	26	27	28	29

MAY
M	T	W	T	F	S	S
	1	2	3	4	5	6
7	8	9	10	11	12	13
14	15	16	17	18	19	20
21	22	23	24	25	26	27
28	29	30	31			

JUNE
M	T	W	T	F	S	S
				1	2	3
4	5	6	7	8	9	10
11	12	13	14	15	16	17
18	19	20	21	22	23	24
25	26	27	28	29	30	

JULY
M	T	W	T	F	S	S
30	31					1
2	3	4	5	6	7	8
9	10	11	12	13	14	15
16	17	18	19	20	21	22
23	24	25	26	27	28	29

AUGUST
M	T	W	T	F	S	S
		1	2	3	4	5
6	7	8	9	10	11	12
13	14	15	16	17	18	19
20	21	22	23	24	25	26
27	28	29	30	31		

SEPTEMBER
M	T	W	T	F	S	S
					1	2
3	4	5	6	7	8	9
10	11	12	13	14	15	16
17	18	19	20	21	22	23
24	25	26	27	28	29	30

OCTOBER
M	T	W	T	F	S	S
1	2	3	4	5	6	7
8	9	10	11	12	13	14
15	16	17	18	19	20	21
22	23	24	25	26	27	28
29	30	31				

NOVEMBER
M	T	W	T	F	S	S
			1	2	3	4
5	6	7	8	9	10	11
12	13	14	15	16	17	18
19	20	21	22	23	24	25
26	27	28	29	30		

DECEMBER
M	T	W	T	F	S	S
31					1	2
3	4	5	6	7	8	9
10	11	12	13	14	15	16
17	18	19	20	21	22	23
24	25	26	27	28	29	30

January

MON
27

TUE
28

WED
29

THU
30

FRI
31

SAT
1
New Year's Day
Daniel Awarded MBE In Queen'
New Year Honours List (2002)

SUN
2

JANUARY

M	T	W	T	F	S	S
					1	2
3	4	5	6	7	8	9
10	11	12	13	14	15	16
17	18	19	20	21	22	23
24	25	26	27	28	29	30
31						

JANUARY

M	T	W	T	F	S	S
					1	2
3	4	5	6	7	8	9
10	11	12	13	14	15	16
17	18	19	20	21	22	23
24	25	26	27	28	29	30
31						

January

Holiday (UK, R of Ireland, AUS, NZL)   MON 3

Holiday (NZL, SCT)   TUE 4

WED 5

THU 6

FRI 7

SAT 8

SUN 9

January

MON
10

TUE
11

WED
12

THU
13

FRI
14

SAT
15

SUN
16

JANUARY

M	T	W	T	F	S	S
					1	2
3	4	5	6	7	8	9
10	11	12	13	14	15	16
17	18	19	20	21	22	23
24	25	26	27	28	29	30
31						

JANUARY

M	T	W	T	F	S	S
					1	2
3	4	5	6	7	8	9
10	11	12	13	14	15	16
17	18	19	20	21	22	23
24	25	26	27	28	29	30
31						

January

Martin Luther King, Jr. Day (Holiday USA)

MON
17

TUE
18

WED
19

THU
20

FRI
21

SAT
22

SUN
23

January

MON
24

TUE
25   Burns Night (SCT)

WED
26   Australia Day (Holiday AUS)

THU
27

FRI
28

SAT
29

SUN
30

JANUARY

M	T	W	T	F	S	S
					1	2
3	4	5	6	7	8	9
10	11	12	13	14	15	16
17	18	19	20	21	22	23
24	25	26	27	28	29	30
31						

Photography by Donna Bachman

FEBRUARY

M	T	W	T	F	S	S
	1	2	3	4	5	6
7	8	9	10	11	12	13
14	15	16	17	18	19	20
21	22	23	24	25	26	27
28						

February

MON
31

TUE
1

WED
2

THU
3

FRI
4

SAT
5

Waitangi Day (Holiday NZL)

SUN
6

February

MON
7

TUE
8

WED
9

First Daniel Recording: 'My Donegal Shore/Stand Beside Me' (1983)

THU
10

FRI
11

SAT
12

SUN
13

FEBRUARY

M	T	W	T	F	S	S
	1	2	3	4	5	6
7	8	9	10	11	12	13
14	15	16	17	18	19	20
21	22	23	24	25	26	27
28						

FEBRUARY

M	T	W	T	F	S	S
		1	2	3	4	5	6
7	8	9	10	11	12	13
14	15	16	17	18	19	20
21	22	23	24	25	26	27
28						

February

St Valentine's Day

MON
14

TUE
15

WED
16

THU
17

FRI
18

SAT
19

SUN
20

February

MON
21   Washington's Birthday (Holiday USA)

TUE
22

WED
23

THU
24

FRI
25

SAT
26

SUN
27

Photography by Donna Bachman

FEBRUARY

M	T	W	T	F	S	S
	1	2	3	4	5	6
7	8	9	10	11	12	13
14	15	16	17	18	19	20
21	22	23	24	25	26	27
28						

MARCH

M	T	W	T	F	S	S
		1	2	3	4	5	6
7	8	9	10	11	12	13
14	15	16	17	18	19	20
21	22	23	24	25	26	27
28	29	30	31			

March

MON
28

St David's Day

TUE
1

WED
2

THU
3

FRI
4

SAT
5

SUN
6

March

MON
7

TUE
8
Shrove Tuesday

WED
9

THU
10
Daniel The Subject Of 'This Is Your Life', BBC TV, 2000

FRI
11

SAT
12

SUN
13
Daylight Saving Time begins (CAN, USA)

MARCH

M	T	W	T	F	S	S
	1	2	3	4	5	6
7	8	9	10	11	12	13
14	15	16	17	18	19	20
21	22	23	24	25	26	27
28	29	30	31			

MARCH

M	T	W	T	F	S	S
	1	2	3	4	5	6
7	8	9	10	11	12	13
14	15	16	17	18	19	20
21	22	23	24	25	26	27
28	29	30	31			

March

Commonwealth Day

MON
14

TUE
15

WED
16

St Patrick's Day
(Holiday R of Ireland, N Ireland)

THU
17

FRI
18

SAT
19

SUN
20

March

MON
21

TUE
22

WED
23

THU
24

FRI
25

SAT
26

SUN
27

British Summer Time begins
European Daylight Saving Time begins

Photography by Donna Bachman

MARCH

M	T	W	T	F	S	S
		1	2	3	4	5	6
7	8	9	10	11	12	13
14	15	16	17	18	19	20
21	22	23	24	25	26	27
28	29	30	31			

MARCH

M	T	W	T	F	S	S
		1	2	3	4	5	6
7	8	9	10	11	12	13
14	15	16	17	18	19	20
21	22	23	24	25	26	27
28	29	30	31			

March

MON 28

Daniel's Highest UK Album Chart Entry To Date, 'Daniel In Blue Jeans', No 3, 2003

TUE 29

WED 30

THU 31

FRI 1

SAT 2

SUN 3

Mother's Day (UK, Ireland)

Daylight Saving Time ends
(NZL, AUS - except WA, NT, QLD)

April

MON
4

TUE
5

WED
6

THU
7

FRI
8

SAT
9

SUN
10

APRIL

M	T	W	T	F	S	S
				1	2	3
4	5	6	7	8	9	10
11	12	13	14	15	16	17
18	19	20	21	22	23	24
25	26	27	28	29	30	

APRIL

M	T	W	T	F	S	S
				1	2	3
4	5	6	7	8	9	10
11	12	13	14	15	16	17
18	19	20	21	22	23	24
25	26	27	28	29	30	

April

Daniel's Highest UK
Singles Chart Entry. 'Give
A Little Love' No 7, 1998

MON
11

TUE
12

WED
13

THU
14

FRI
15

SAT
16

SUN
17

April

MON
18

TUE
19

WED
20

THU
21

FRI
22

Good Friday (Holiday UK, AUS, CAN, NZL)
Earth Day

SAT
23

St George's Day

SUN
24

Easter Sunday

APRIL

M	T	W	T	F	S	S
				1	2	3
4	5	6	7	8	9	10
11	12	13	14	15	16	17
18	19	20	21	22	23	24
25	26	27	28	29	30	

APRIL

M	T	W	T	F	S	S
				1	2	3
4	5	6	7	8	9	10
11	12	13	14	15	16	17
18	19	20	21	22	23	24
25	26	27	28	29	30	

April

MON 25
Easter Monday (Holiday UK except SCT, R of Ireland, AUS, NZL)
Anzac Day

TUE 26

WED 27

THU 28

FRI 29

SAT 30

SUN 1

May

MON   Holiday (UK, R of Ireland)
2

TUE
3

WED
4

THU
5

FRI
6

SAT
7

SUN   Mother's Day (AUS, CAN, NZL, USA)
8

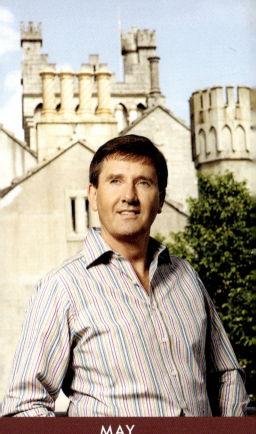

MAY

M	T	W	T	F	S	S
						1
2	3	4	5	6	7	8
9	10	11	12	13	14	15
16	17	18	19	20	21	22
23	24	25	26	27	28	29
30	31					

MAY

M	T	W	T	F	S	S
						1
2	3	4	5	6	7	8
9	10	11	12	13	14	15
16	17	18	19	20	21	22
23	24	25	26	27	28	29
30	31					

May

MON
9

TUE
10

WED
11

THU
12

FRI
13

SAT
14

SUN
15

May

MON
16

TUE
17

WED
18

THU
19

FRI
20

SAT
21

SUN
22

Daniel's First Concert At The
Carnegie Hall, New York, 1991

MAY

M	T	W	T	F	S	S
						1
2	3	4	5	6	7	8
9	10	11	12	13	14	15
16	17	18	19	20	21	22
23	24	25	26	27	28	29
30	31					

Photography by Donna Bachman

MAY

M	T	W	T	F	S	S
						1
2	3	4	5	6	7	8
9	10	11	12	13	14	15
16	17	18	19	20	21	22
23	24	25	26	27	28	29
30	31					

May

Victoria Day (Holiday CAN)

MON
23

TUE
24

WED
25

THU
26

FRI
27

SAT
28

SUN
29

May

MON
30

Holiday (UK)
Memorial Day (Holiday USA)

TUE
31

WED
1

THU
2

FRI
3

SAT
4

SUN
5

JUNE

M	T	W	T	F	S	S
				1	2	3
				1	2	3

M	T	W	T	F	S	S
	1	2	3	4	5	
6	7	8	9	10	11	12
13	14	15	16	17	18	19
20	21	22	23	24	25	26
27	28	29	30			

JUNE

M	T	W	T	F	S	S
			1	2	3	4	5
6	7	8	9	10	11	12
13	14	15	16	17	18	19
20	21	22	23	24	25	26
27	28	29	30			

June

Queen's Birthday (Holiday NZL)
Holiday (R of Ireland)

MON 6

TUE 7

WED 8

THU 9

FRI 10

Daniel Honoured By
The Variety Club Of
Great Britain, 1996

SAT 11

SUN 12

June

MON
13

TUE
14

WED
15

THU
16

FRI
17

SAT
18

SUN
19   Father's Day (UK, CAN, USA)

Photography by Donna Bachman

JUNE

M	T	W	T	F	S	S
		1	2	3	4	5
6	7	8	9	10	11	12
13	14	15	16	17	18	19
20	21	22	23	24	25	26
27	28	29	30			

JUNE

M	T	W	T	F	S	S
			1	2	3	4	5
6	7	8	9	10	11	12
13	14	15	16	17	18	19
20	21	22	23	24	25	26
27	28	29	30			

June

MON
20

TUE
21

WED
22

THU
23

FRI
24

SAT
25

SUN
26

June

MON
27

TUE
28

WED
29

THU
30

FRI
1
Canada Day (Holiday CAN)

SAT
2

SUN
3

JULY

M	T	W	T	F	S	S
				1	2	3
4	5	6	7	8	9	10
11	12	13	14	15	16	17
18	19	20	21	22	23	24
25	26	27	28	29	30	31

Photography by Donna Bochman

JULY

M	T	W	T	F	S	S
				1	2	3
4	5	6	7	8	9	10
11	12	13	14	15	16	17
18	19	20	21	22	23	24
25	26	27	28	29	30	31

July

Independence Day (Holiday USA) — **MON 4**

TUE 5

WED 6

THU 7

FRI 8

SAT 9

SUN 10

July

MON
11
Daniel's First Concert At The Point, Dublin, 1992

TUE
12
Battle of the Boyne (Holiday N Ireland)

WED
13

THU
14

FRI
15

SAT
16

SUN
17

JULY

M	T	W	T	F	S	S
				1	2	3
4	5	6	7	8	9	10
11	12	13	14	15	16	17
18	19	20	21	22	23	24
25	26	27	28	29	30	31

JULY

M	T	W	T	F	S	S
				1	2	3
4	5	6	7	8	9	10
11	12	13	14	15	16	17
18	19	20	21	22	23	24
25	26	27	28	29	30	31

July

MON
18

TUE
19

WED
20

THU
21

FRI
22

SAT
23

SUN
24

July

MON
25

TUE
26

WED
27

THU
28

FRI
29

SAT
30

SUN
31

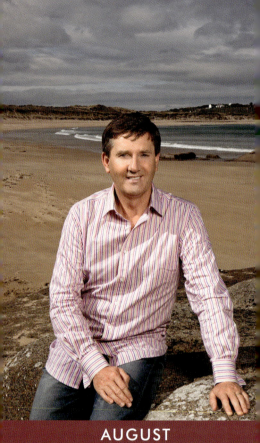

AUGUST

M	T	W	T	F	S	S
1	2	3	4	5	6	7
8	9	10	11	12	13	14
15	16	17	18	19	20	21
22	23	24	25	26	27	28
29	30	31				

August

MON 1 — Holiday (Scotland, R of Ireland)

TUE 2

WED 3

THU 4

FRI 5

SAT 6

SUN 7

August

MON
8

TUE
9

WED
10

THU
11

FRI
12

SAT
13

Daniel's First Irish No.1 Single, 'Take Good Care Of Her', 1987

SUN
14

AUGUST

M	T	W	T	F	S	S
	1	2	3	4	5	6	7
8	9	10	11	12	13	14
15	16	17	18	19	20	21
22	23	24	25	26	27	28
29	30	31				

AUGUST

M	T	W	T	F	S	S
	1	2	3	4	5	6	7
8	9	10	11	12	13	14
15	16	17	18	19	20	21
22	23	24	25	26	27	28
29	30	31				

August

MON
15

TUE
16

WED
17

THU
18

FRI
19

SAT
20

SUN
21

August

MON
22

TUE
23

WED
24

THU
25

FRI
26

SAT
27

SUN
28

AUGUST

M	T	W	T	F	S	S
	1	2	3	4	5	6	7
8	9	10	11	12	13	14
15	16	17	18	19	20	21
22	23	24	25	26	27	28
29	30	31				

AUGUST

M	T	W	T	F	S	S
1	2	3	4	5	6	7
8	9	10	11	12	13	14
15	16	17	18	19	20	21
22	23	24	25	26	27	28
29	30	31				

August

Holiday (UK except SCT)

MON 29

TUE 30

WED 31

THU 1

FRI 2

SAT 3

Father's Day (AUS, NZL)

SUN 4

September

MON
5
Labor Day (Holiday USA)
Labour Day (Holiday CAN)

TUE
6

WED
7

THU
8

FRI
9

SAT
10

SUN
11

SEPTEMBER

M	T	W	T	F	S	S
			1	2	3	4
5	6	7	8	9	10	11
12	13	14	15	16	17	18
19	20	21	22	23	24	25
26	27	28	29	30		

SEPTEMBER

M	T	W	T	F	S	S
			1	2	3	4
5	6	7	8	9	10	11
12	13	14	15	16	17	18
19	20	21	22	23	24	25
26	27	28	29	30		

September

MON
12

TUE
13

WED
14

THU
15

FRI
16

Daniel's First Top Of The Pop's Appearance, 'I Just Want To Dance With You', 1992

SAT
17

SUN
18

September

MON
19

TUE
20

WED
21

UN International Day of Peace

THU
22

FRI
23

Daniel's First Appearance At
The Royal Albert Hall, 1988

SAT
24

SUN
25

Daylight Saving Time begins (NZL)

SEPTEMBER

M	T	W	T	F	S	S
			1	2	3	4
5	6	7	8	9	10	11
12	13	14	15	16	17	18
19	20	21	22	23	24	25
26	27	28	29	30		

SEPTEMBER

M	T	W	T	F	S	S
			1	2	3	4
5	6	7	8	9	10	11
12	13	14	15	16	17	18
19	20	21	22	23	24	25
26	27	28	29	30		

September

MON
26

TUE
27

WED
28

THU
29

FRI
30

SAT
1

Daylight Saving Time begins
(AUS - except WA, NT, QLD)

Daniel's First Self-written Album
'Until The Next Time', Released 2006

SUN
2

October

MON
3

TUE
4   World Animal Day

WED
5

THU
6

FRI
7

SAT
8

SUN
9

OCTOBER

M	T	W	T	F	S	S
					1	2
3	4	5	6	7	8	9
10	11	12	13	14	15	16
17	18	19	20	21	22	23
24	25	26	27	28	29	30
31						

OCTOBER

M	T	W	T	F	S	S
					1	2
3	4	5	6	7	8	9
10	11	12	13	14	15	16
17	18	19	20	21	22	23
24	25	26	27	28	29	30
31						

October

Columbus Day (Holiday USA)
Thanksgiving Day (Holiday CAN)

MON
10

TUE
11

WED
12

THU
13

FRI
14

SAT
15

SUN
16

October

MON
17

TUE
18

WED
19

THU
20

FRI
21

SAT
22

SUN
23

OCTOBER

M	T	W	T	F	S	S
					1	2
3	4	5	6	7	8	9
10	11	12	13	14	15	16
17	18	19	20	21	22	23
24	25	26	27	28	29	30
31						

Photography by Diair Whiteman

OCTOBER

M	T	W	T	F	S	S
					1	2
3	4	5	6	7	8	9
10	11	12	13	14	15	16
17	18	19	20	21	22	23
24	25	26	27	28	29	30
31						

October

Labour Day (Holiday NZL)

MON
24

TUE
25

WED
26

THU
27

'Faith & Inspiration' enters UK
Album Charts, No 4, 2000

FRI
28

SAT
29

British Summer Time ends
European Daylight Saving time ends

SUN
30

November

MON
31
Holiday (R of Ireland)
Hallowe'en

TUE
1

WED
2

THU
3

FRI
4
Daniel & Majella's
Wedding, 2002

SAT
5
Bonfire Night

SUN
6
Daylight Saving Time ends (CAN, USA)

NOVEMBER

M	T	W	T	F	S	S
	1	2	3	4	5	6
7	8	9	10	11	12	13
14	15	16	17	18	19	20
21	22	23	24	25	26	27
28	29	30				

NOVEMBER

M	T	W	T	F	S	S
		1	2	3	4	5	6
7	8	9	10	11	12	13
14	15	16	17	18	19	20
21	22	23	24	25	26	27
28	29	30				

November

MON 7

TUE 8

WED 9

THU 10

Veterans' Day (Holiday USA)
Remembrance Day (Holiday CAN)

FRI 11

SAT 12

Remembrance Sunday (UK)

SUN 13

November

MON
14

TUE
15

WED
16

THU
17

FRI
18

SAT
19

SUN
20

NOVEMBER

M	T	W	T	F	S	S
	1	2	3	4	5	6
7	8	9	10	11	12	13
14	15	16	17	18	19	20
21	22	23	24	25	26	27
28	29	30				

NOVEMBER

M	T	W	T	F	S	S
	1	2	3	4	5	6
7	8	9	10	11	12	13
14	15	16	17	18	19	20
21	22	23	24	25	26	27
28	29	30				

November

MON
21

TUE
22

WED
23

Thanksgiving Day (Holiday USA)

THU
24

FRI
25

SAT
26

SUN
27

November

MON
28

TUE
29

WED
30   St Andrew's Day (Holiday SCT)

THU
1

FRI
2

SAT
3

SUN
4

DECEMBER

M	T	W	T	F	S	S
				1	2	3	4
5	6	7	8	9	10	11
12	13	14	15	16	17	18
19	20	21	22	23	24	25
26	27	28	29	30	31	

DECEMBER

M	T	W	T	F	S	S
			1	2	3	4
5	6	7	8	9	10	11
12	13	14	15	16	17	18
19	20	21	22	23	24	25
26	27	28	29	30	31	

December

MON 5

TUE 6

WED 7

THU 8

FRI 9

SAT 10

Daniel Honoured By
The Variety Club Of
Great Britain, 2006

SUN 11

December

MON
12

Daniel's Birthday, 1961,
Star Sign Sagittarius

TUE
13

WED
14

THU
15

FRI
16

SAT
17

SUN
18

DECEMBER

M	T	W	T	F	S	S
				1	2	3	4
5	6	7	8	9	10	11
12	13	14	15	16	17	18
19	20	21	22	23	24	25
26	27	28	29	30	31	

DECEMBER

M	T	W	T	F	S	S
				1	2	3	4
5	6	7	8	9	10	11
12	13	14	15	16	17	18
19	20	21	22	23	24	25
26	27	28	29	30	31	

December

MON
19

TUE
20

WED
21

THU
22

FRI
23

Christmas Eve

SAT
24

Christmas Day

SUN
25

December

MON
26

Boxing Day
(Holiday UK, USA, CAN, AUS, NZL)

TUE
27

Holiday (UK, AUS, NZL, CAN)

WED
28

THU
29

FRI
30

SAT
31

New Year's Eve

SUN
1

New Year's Day

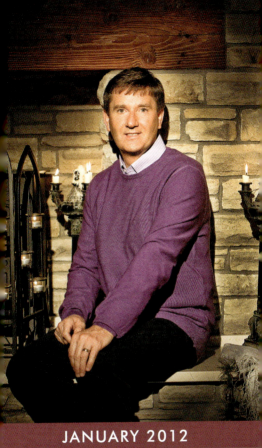

JANUARY 2012

M	T	W	T	F	S	S
						1
2	3	4	5	6	7	8
9	10	11	12	13	14	15
16	17	18	19	20	21	22
23	24	25	26	27	28	29
30	31					

Addresses

Name

Address

....

....

Home tel.

Work tel.

Mobile tel.

Email

Name

Address

....

....

Home tel.

Work tel.

Mobile tel.

Email

Name

Address

....

....

Home tel.

Work tel.

Mobile tel.

Email

Addresses

Name

Address

Home tel.

Work tel.

Mobile tel.

Email

Name

Address

Home tel.

Work tel.

Mobile tel.

Email

Name

Address

Home tel.

Work tel.

Mobile tel.

Email

Addresses

Name
Address

Home tel.
Work tel.
Mobile tel.
Email

Name
Address

Home tel.
Work tel.
Mobile tel.
Email

Name
Address

Home tel.
Work tel.
Mobile tel.
Email

Addresses

Name

Address

Home tel.

Work tel.

Mobile tel.

Email

Name

Address

Home tel.

Work tel.

Mobile tel.

Email

Name

Address

Home tel.

Work tel.

Mobile tel.

Email

Addresses

Name
Address

Home tel.
Work tel.
Mobile tel.
Email

Name
Address

Home tel.
Work tel.
Mobile tel.
Email

Name
Address

Home tel.
Work tel.
Mobile tel.
Email

Addresses

Name

Address

Home tel.

Work tel.

Mobile tel.

Email

Name

Address

Home tel.

Work tel.

Mobile tel.

Email

Name

Address

Home tel.

Work tel.

Mobile tel.

Email

Notes